Meeting the Learning Needs of All Children

Personalised learning involves helping each child to reach his or her full potential – intellectually, personally and socially. To achieve this, teachers need to match learning opportunities to the learning styles and experiences of the children, taking into account individual differences in culture, language, background, ability and interests.

For many teachers, individual learning has always been at the heart of what they do in the classroom. In this book, experienced teacher and author Joan Dean unpicks the concept of personalised learning and shows teachers how to apply it to planning, teaching and assessing learning.

The book is accessibly written and gets right to the nitty-gritty of what personalised learning looks like in the classroom. It covers:

- a whole-school approach to personalised learning;
- getting to know the children;
- working with boys and girls;
- providing for children with special educational needs;
- providing for very able children;
- providing for children from other cultures;
- providing for children for whom English is not their first language;
- providing for children from different social backgrounds;
- working with assistants and volunteers.

Joan Dean has been a teacher and a head teacher with experience in primary, secondary, further and higher education. She has also worked as a teacher trainer, primary schools adviser, chief inspector and school governor and has lectured widely in the UK and abroad. She was awarded an OBE in 1980 for services to education.

Meeting the Learning Needs of All Children

Personalised learning in the primary school

Joan Dean

Routledge
Taylor & Francis Group

LONDON AND NEW YORK

First published 2006 by Routledge
2 Park Square, Milton Park, Abingdon, Oxon OX14 4RN

Simultaneously published in the USA and Canada
by Routledge
270 Madison Avenue, New York, NY 10016

Routledge is an imprint of the Taylor & Francis Group, an informa business

© 2006 Joan Dean

Typeset in Times New Roman and Gill by
Florence Production Ltd, Stoodleigh, Devon
Printed and bound in Great Britain by
Bell & Bain Ltd, Glasgow

British Library Cataloguing in Publication Data
A catalogue record for this book is available from the British Library

Library of Congress Cataloging in Publication Data
A catalog record has been requested for this book

ISBN10: 0–415–39427–9

ISBN13: 978–0–415–39427–7

Contents

Abbreviations   vi

1 What is personalised learning?   1

2 A whole-school approach to personalised learning   7

3 The children   12

4 Learning and teaching   20

5 Providing for boys and girls   29

6 Children with special educational needs   35

7 Working with very able children   45

8 Children from other cultures   52

9 Children from different social backgrounds   58

10 Personal, social and health education   62

11 Working with support staff and volunteers   67

12 Working with parents   72

13 Staff development   76

14 School self-evaluation   81

15 Conclusion   86

References   87
Index   88

Abbreviations

ADHD	attention deficit hyperactivity disorder
EAL	English as an additional language
EMAG	Ethnic Minority Achievement Grant
GCSE	General Certificate of Secondary Education
ICT	information and communications technology
IDP	Individual Development Plan
ILP	Individual Learning Plan
ISP	Intensified Support Programme
IQ	intelligence quotient
LEA	local education authority
LSA	learning support assistant
NVQ	National Vocational Qualification
P levels	Levels of attainment below the National Curriculum levels
PDC	professional development coordinator
PDM	professional development meeting
PSHE	personal, social and health education
PTA	parent/teacher association
RAP	raising attainment plan
SATs	Standard Attainment Tasks
SEN	special educational needs
SENCO	special educational needs coordinator

Chapter 1

What is personalised learning?

Personalised learning is a term that has been much used by government and in professional circles recently and is something with which teachers are now becoming familiar. What does it mean to you, the class teacher of a primary school class, and what does it mean to the staff of the school in which you work?

Personalised learning is education that sets out to meet the needs and abilities of every individual pupil. There is a sense in which good teachers have always tried to do this, but there is now a greater emphasis on it and it has become a more possible goal with the advent of teaching assistants and the use of information and communication technology (ICT). Personalised learning involves trying to assess the learning needs and learning styles of every child and tailoring lessons to meet those needs by using a range of approaches, choices and teaching styles to match them. An important element in personalised learning is that children are encouraged to make decisions about their own learning from quite an early age and, where appropriate, this may mean offering a choice of activities within lessons. Children also need to learn to make decisions about how they learn, thus opportunities for different learning styles need to be provided. This also means that there needs to be an element of choice in learning and that children need to be made aware of their own learning styles.

In a school where there is personalised learning teachers will work together to learn themselves and cooperate to provide for children's learning. The school will also involve parents a good deal and may cooperate with other schools pursuing the same agenda.

Personalised learning is about children and their development. Each child will come to school with different experiences, different inheritance of genes, different abilities and different potential. Some will have developed positive self-esteem and have the belief that they can achieve. Others may have a less positive view of themselves and will need to be given confidence in their abilities. Some will have learnt a great deal at home and in nursery education. Others will start at an earlier stage of learning. Some will have learned to behave well and be considerate to other people. Others may have had little contact outside the home and have much to learn about good social behaviour. There will also be children who start with a disadvantage because of a disability or because they speak very little English. The teacher needs to get to know all of them as individuals, assessing what they each can do and differentiating work according to the needs of individuals, so providing opportunities for them all to learn.

Personalised education is about helping children to become sensitive and balanced individuals who have a positive view of themselves, good human beings who care for others and can relate well to them. Of course, parents have a primary role in this, but school also plays a very important part. We need to respect children as individuals who need to grow and learn, using their talents to the full, relating well to others, developing a positive self-image and a belief that they can succeed if they try hard enough. This means that teachers have to ensure that the demands made on children match their abilities, giving each one a chance to succeed. It is important to build on the strengths of individuals as well as working to improve areas of weakness.

It is also important that the culture of each child is respected and that the child is helped to feel proud of his or her background. The range of cultural backgrounds in the school may be considerable. There may not only be children from different races, often speaking different languages, but also children from different social backgrounds. As a teacher you need to be as familiar as you can be with the children's backgrounds and at the same time be concerned to induct all of them into the prevailing British culture, which is to a large extent white and middle-class. Children from disadvantaged homes need to learn standard English so that they would have an equal chance in the job market later on. Children from other races may have different social customs at home; teachers need to be aware of these as far as they are able because of the possibility of misunderstanding, but the children will also need to learn British social customs. All this learning needs to be introduced in ways that do not imply to children that their home culture is less valid and important but rather that there is also a culture that they need to share with the wider community.

Independent learning

Personalised learning is also about becoming independent as a learner and as a person. Many of the skills with which education is concerned contribute to this aim. Primary school children gradually learn independence and develop the ability to do things for themselves as they grow, and we need to encourage this. The ability to read gives a person freedom to access different views and ideas, but children also require the ability to read intelligently, selecting what is relevant to a given end, so helping children to ask questions about what they read and to seek replies is important. They need to learn to judge their own performance against appropriate criteria that they have been involved in defining and have accepted. Their ability to do this will gradually develop throughout the primary years, and teachers need to be concerned with helping them to learn the skills of independent learning. Children also have much to learn about making relationships and trying to see another person's point of view. Emotional development is an important area for learning: children need to learn to manage their emotions.

Creativity

It is important for each child's development to encourage creativity. This is not simply a matter of the so-called creative subjects such as art, music, English and technology but also a concern with encouraging children to think of ideas and be able to develop them – and this should be part of work in all subjects. You need to ask yourself from time to time whether you are doing enough to develop ideas, perhaps asking the children for ideas, such as how many different ways can they think of to solve a mathematical problem, what they imagine life was like for children in a past society or another place, or how they can test an idea in science. The creative person will have an approach to life that finds solutions to problems of everyday living and enjoyment in creating things.

Differentiating work

Primary school teachers have for many years been concerned to try to match their teaching to the needs of individuals and to differentiate work according to individual need. This is the other aspect of personalised learning that teachers need to take on board. It is not easy, particularly when classes are large and contain a wide variety of children. Children will be at different stages of development, and this needs to be taken into account when planning work. In many primary school classes there will be children with special educational needs at a variety of levels, possibly including some with quite serious problems. There may be children from different cultures and ethnic groups, some of whom may start school with very little English. There may also be some very able children who will make considerable demands upon teachers if they are to provide work for them that challenges their ability and maintains their interest. There will probably be some children who pose behaviour problems and perhaps some children from homes where they are not encouraged to learn. Most primary classes also contain both boys and girls who learn in different ways and make different demands on the teacher. While this variety may be stimulating, it is also very demanding. This diversity makes it very important to assess the abilities, attitudes and learning style of each child and to plan so that the teaching may be appropriate for them all. This is a tall order!

Support for personalised learning

There is now some appreciation of the demands made on primary teachers and this has led to the appointment of a number of teaching assistants and also learning support assistants (LSAs) to work with children with special needs. The greater provision of ICT in schools is also a help, in that records can be kept online and children can search the internet and can work with electronic lessons in some cases. Teachers can also access some lesson plans, and teachers taking the same year group can perhaps share planning by putting their plans on computer. The school can also create banks of ideas for particular areas of teaching and learning, which teachers can develop and build up over a period. The provision and use of ICT is likely to develop further, and in the future there will be more online that can help teachers, who will sometimes be in more of a support role, helping children to access suitable material and learn individually from a range of programmes. These will probably include some programmes made by the staff of the school and available to everyone who needs them. Computers can make personalised learning for all children a genuine possibility.

Personalised education does not mean that all learning should be individual. That would not only be nearly impossible but also a waste of the learning opportunities that occur when children work together and learn from each other. The Literacy and Numeracy Strategies and the Primary Strategy recognised that teachers could work with a whole class and still reach individuals within it if they planned for this. The task is one of making long-term plans, for groups of children and for some individuals, that are specific and can be assessed, and then looking carefully at what you plan each day and week in the light of those long-term plans.

Acquiring learning skills

A very important task for all teachers is to help children to acquire learning skills. Each piece of work demands particular skills, and these can be discussed with children. As teacher you need to be clear in your own mind how children will demonstrate that they have acquired each particular skill and plan work carefully so that the skills can be introduced as children seem ready for them. Children should also be made aware of the learning skills they are acquiring and appreciate when and how they should be used. They will need to learn discussion skills so that they can learn from each other. Wegerif and Dawes (2004) describe small groups of children discussing a problem posed by a computer and then learning to present a point of view and discuss its relevance to the problem. Children also need skill in using reading to learn, and older children can learn to make notes from what they read. They need to develop skill in organising their ideas in order to present them in writing or orally.

Target-setting

The process of providing for individuals within the class starts with an assessment of where each child is in his or her learning, and this will serve as a basis for future planning.

The task is one of making long-term plans for grouping children and for some individuals, which are specific and can be assessed. The discussion needs to involve suggestions from you or the child about how the targets might be achieved and how they will be assessed. These will be targets in different areas of curriculum according to the needs and stage of development of the child. Some of these targets will be in curriculum areas and will be part of your overall objectives, and some may be targets for acquiring learning skills; there may also be behavioural objectives for some children. Each child could have a record book in which the targets and the date for their achievement are recorded. At the end of the target period, which could be different for each child, you could check on how well the child has done and sign, date and comment in the record book. This process is described in more detail in Chapter 4.

More general targets

Not all work can be presented simply in terms of specific targets. You also need to be concerned with outcomes, which you need to think about when you set the targets. If you teach older children, for example, you may want children to learn how to make notes from reading, and you will have to make judgements about how well an individual is doing in this. You may want children to develop skill in presentation, writing, drawing and ICT, and in talking to the class. You may be looking at skills such as the ability to play or work with others. This will be particularly relevant when you are working with younger children, who need to learn these skills at an early stage so that they can use them well as they grow older. These are all areas – and there are many others – where you can make the children aware of the skills you want them to acquire and then find ways of making judgements about their success, perhaps involving other children in helping to make these judgements. It is important in all these cases to involve children in thinking about the skills they need to acquire so that they feel some ownership of them.

A child making a presentation to the class might benefit from positive comments from other children. You might ask the class what was good about the presentation, being careful to avoid damaging a child's confidence. You then need to look for pointers to development to discuss with the child individually. Children might also be asked to make judgements about each other's work, perhaps in pairs, emphasising the importance of telling your partner what is good about the work. This sort of activity helps children to be aware of the criteria by which your judgements are made and so helps them to be able to judge their own work. It is also useful to ask children to judge their own work from time to time, again helping them to become aware of the criteria you want them to use. The plans may be for a small group, a pair or an individual, but sometimes they will be plans for the whole class, which will run alongside individual plans.

Case study

Janet, the class teacher of a Year 5 class, was concerned about how few boys appeared to enjoy reading. She wanted to persuade the boys – and the girls, too – to read more and to get more pleasure from reading. She decided to place stress on personal reading. The school had a good library so there were plenty of books to choose from, both fiction and non-fiction. She gave each child a notebook in which to record the books they read, and she encouraged them to make some comment about each book, saying what they had enjoyed. She provided a small amount of time for children to read during the school day, though it was difficult to fit this in. She also encouraged them to read at odd times during the day such as when she was taking the register.

continued

She talked to the whole class about books that she thought they might like and stressed particularly those that she thought boys might like. She noted the books that the children had said they enjoyed and asked some of them, particularly boys but some girls as well, to talk to the class about these books. She made a point of introducing some non-fiction books that she thought boys might enjoy as well as some that girls would like, and this paid dividends. She arranged for a number of exhibitions of library books that she thought children might like. She talked about these and pointed out books that she thought different children might enjoy. She asked children who had enjoyed a particular book to write something about it so that other people could decide if they would like to read it. They made a display of these comments so that everyone could see the recommendations.

She also encouraged children to aim at reading a certain number of books by the end of term. This could be different for different children but she encouraged them to set the largest number that they felt they could read if they really made an effort. This gave them something to aim for, and they recorded their targets in their record books and also their progress towards them.

Overall the children's interest in reading increased, and both boys and girls said they now enjoyed reading much more.

Learning styles and learning targets

You also need to be aware of each child's learning style. While it is probably counter-productive to try to meet all the possible different styles, it is useful know that John learns best from things he can see and finds learning from books a bit of a chore. Marilyn, on other hand, loves to read and explore ideas from books. Still other children may learn best when they are active. You need to bear all these styles in mind in planning work and try to provide opportunities for learning in different ways.

A programme of this kind will take time to set up, and it will be important to think about children's targets, both for individuals and for groups, when you plan work for the whole class. For example, with a Year 4 class, you might plan a study of the local environment. The plans for the whole class might involve learning the names of different plants and trees in the school grounds and making a map of the locality and a plan of the school. You may want some children to learn about how to find and use information in books, and they can be asked to look up the trees and plants they find and draw and write about their findings for a classroom display. You will need to work with them on the skills involved in making notes and discuss ways of selecting the important points and then saying something very briefly.

The use of space

Perhaps two or three children need help in measuring and setting out plans of the school. Such a programme might also involve interviewing people in the area and finding out about the history of the various buildings and perhaps asking parents or grandparents about what it was like in the area when they were young. This will involve learning interviewing skills.

Social skills

Another area of learning that involves the acquisition of skills is that of social competence. Children need to learn to work together, sharing and taking turns and learning to see from the other person's point of view. They need the skills of empathy, and in particular they need to learn to manage their own emotions. At all stages in a primary school there is a need to include learning about emotional development, learning to control one's feelings of anger and irritation, feelings about other people's behaviour. Children need to discover how they can control strong feelings and how they can deal with others who are feeling full of emotion. Drama and role play may be helpful here, with children considering situations that stimulate strong feelings and looking for ways to cope with their own feelings and those expressed by others.

A programme of the kind set out in this chapter will probably need a good many resources. It may need well thought-out worksheets and a range of books and other resources to match the needs of the children concerned. It needs varied teaching approaches so that the needs of all children are met. It will work more effectively if you share ideas with other teachers as part of a whole-school programme for providing personalised learning.

Questions to think about

1   What do I know about my children's individual learning styles and learning needs? How can I make use of this information?

2   How can I assess individual learning styles?

3   Do I vary my teaching approaches to provide for all the children? Do I encourage creativity?

4   Am I giving the children opportunities for making decisions about some of their work?

5   What learning skills do I want my children to develop? How can I create opportunities for this?

6   What targets should I set for work with my class and what targets should I set for individual children?

7   How many of my children have a positive self-image? What can I do for others who tend to have a negative view of their abilities?

8   What can I do to encourage children to develop good social behaviour? What social behaviour do I want to see?

9   How can I best cater for the range of children in my class? What do I need to do for boys and girls, children from ethnic minorities, for children learning English, for very able children, for children with special needs, for children from disadvantaged homes?

Chapter 2

A whole-school approach to personalised learning

While it is possible for an individual teacher to develop a personalised learning programme in his or her own classroom, it is much more likely to be successful if there is a whole-school approach. The school needs to have a vision of what personalised learning is all about that has been discussed and agreed by all staff. The vision needs to be widely shared and to be based on shared values.

Important among these values will be the idea of equal opportunities for all children and the inclusion of all children and all staff in the activities of the school. Inclusion is about providing a framework in which all children can be valued equally. Inclusion must be concerned with how children see their gender, ethnicity, abilities and social background to be perceived by peers and by staff, and it is important to help children develop positive views of their own characteristics and abilities. Staff need to think carefully about how this can be achieved. It does not mean treating everyone alike, but rather demonstrating that every child is valued. Many of us have elements of prejudice about people of different ethnic and social groups that we are reluctant to recognise but nevertheless affect the way we behave from time to time. Staff need to be very watchful to make sure that hidden prejudice does not affect the way they deal with children. In particular, stereotyping of black Afro-Caribbean boys as trouble-makers is shown by research to be more common than most teachers would like to think.

Consideration of common values leads to a definition of vision for the school. Having an agreed vision will help to ensure that everyone agrees on the fundamental values and priorities. It gives a framework for school policies and helps to ensure that everyone is working in a similar direction towards common goals. The vision needs to be concerned with behaviour, relationships and the valuing of all members of the school community as well as more academic learning and the celebration of diversity. Personal, social and health education is an important area; it will be dealt with partly as incidents arise that lead to discussion of ways of behaving towards other people and partly through a planned programme (see Chapter 10). The vision needs to be shared in appropriate ways with the children and their parents, who need to feel that they are part of the process of developing the vision. Vision should not be something planned, discussed and then forgotten. It needs to be returned to regularly, with staff asking of any development: 'How does this reflect our vision for the school?' Head teachers need constantly to work to keep the vision before their colleagues.

Culture and climate

An agreed vision for the school leads to a particular school culture, a sense of 'this is the way we do things here', and this should be in the minds of both staff and children. The vision to some extent defines the culture and the climate that results from it. An important aspect of this for the staff is the extent to which they work together and support each other in working out problems in a collegial way. There is not only a school climate but a climate in each classroom, created by the teacher who works there. It is desirable that the climate in individual classrooms not only reflects the personality and style of the individual teacher but also reflects the school culture and climate. The more teachers work together the more likely it is that there will be a common climate across the school.

It is the children who will be aware of the classroom climate. Do they find learning enjoyable for much of the time? Or do they spend time trying to guess what answer the teacher wants? Are they hesitant about answering a question in case they get it wrong in front of the rest of the class? Are they sure about what they may do and must not do? Do they have a sense of belonging to a community – the community of the class and of the school? There is much to be said for teachers making a survey of children's views of what happens in the classroom (see Chapter 4).

Another aspect of culture and climate is the hidden curriculum. What do the children learn that the teacher does not intend? Do they get the impression that boys are more important than girls because the teacher asks boys more questions than girls? Or do they believe that black children are less intelligent than white children? Have they the idea that English and maths are more important than any other subjects? Would the teacher be surprised that children had these views? Are there any other areas in which there is a hidden curriculum of which staff are not aware? A teaching assistant, particularly one new to the school, may see or hear things that the teacher does not know about and may benefit from hearing.

Planning for school improvement

The staff of a school that is planning to make learning more personalised need to start by discussing it together, considering how learning could be better matched to the needs of individual children and how, as teachers and assistants, they can continue to develop their own knowledge and skills. Teachers will certainly have ideas about this and can start to consider what a classroom where learning is personalised as far as possible would actually look like. A head teacher who spends time observing in classrooms should be able to call on different members of staff who have made moves in this direction to tell the group about how any practices they are currently using contribute to the learning and development of individual children. It should be stressed that personalised learning is not about making all teaching and learning individual. It is rather about being concerned with the needs of individual children, knowing children's strengths and areas in which they need to develop and planning work for the class that takes individual needs into account.

If a school is going to develop an inclusive and personalised education for its children, there will be a need for good planning. Development planning has been part of good practice for some time and this involves regularly asking questions such as the following:

- How well are we doing? What evidence is there of improving standards? Are we succeeding in making the education we offer our children more personalised? Are we meeting the needs of all groups and individuals? Answering these questions requires a careful survey of what is happening at present which leads into the next question.
- How well should we be doing? What more can we aim to achieve? What are our strengths and in what areas should we be able to do better? With which children are we not succeeding? How can we best help them?
- What must we do to improve? This is the stage for making an action plan, setting objectives and defining criteria for success, and also agreeing how success is going to be monitored and by whom.

Staff development

Personalised learning is not something just for the children. It applies to the staff as well. The school needs to be a learning community in which all staff are concerned with learning, their own as well as the children's, and in which people identify the areas in which they want to learn and are supported by colleagues as they learn. This is something that the staff – both teachers and support staff – need to do together, supporting and helping each other, learning from each other and working as a team.

Staff considering such a development need to think about the professional development required and about the personal learning each person will need in order to implement the idea. There may also be local courses that are relevant, and staff attending such courses can give feedback to colleagues. Reading will also be valuable, and different people can arrange to read particular books or papers and give feedback. The discussion and joint planning that can take place at an in-service day will be very important since if the plan is to succeed, it needs commitment from everyone.

Arrangements can also be made for teachers to visit each other's classrooms, in pairs or in small groups, perhaps at lunch time or after school, to see the provision that is being made and to discuss their findings; if time can be found for it, visiting other schools for ideas can also be arranged.

It is also useful to consider how children can be consulted about how they think they learn best, perhaps asking older children to complete questionnaires on this and talking about it with groups of both younger and older children (see Chapter 4). These ideas can be discussed, and a way forward for the whole school can start to take shape.

It should also be possible to think about ways in which teachers can cooperate to develop more personalised work, if possible taking time to observe each other teaching and discuss their findings. This is not very easy to arrange but is valuable for both the observer and the observed. The Primary Strategy suggests an intensified support programme (ISP) with the school planning a strategy and programme for raising attainment. It identifies as key themes for such a programme:

- raising standards and accelerating progress;
- improving the quality of teaching and learning;
- improving the conditions for learning;
- developing as a professional community.

These are themes that the school will benefit from adopting.

In this programme there should be a professional development meeting (PDM) each half-term attended by all teachers and teaching assistants, at which aims for the half-term are reviewed. Each teacher sets targets for his or her own class for the coming half-term and makes an individual development plan (IDP), and ways of addressing the targets are discussed. Where there is more than one class in a year group the teachers concerned can share ideas.

At a similar meeting the following half-term, each teacher first reports on how his or her work has gone and then goes on to agree new targets for the coming half-term. Teachers of the same or consecutive year groups might plan some work together, each contributing ideas about how to make the learning match the needs of the children. They might also sometimes exchange children in order to provide for the range of abilities and needs, perhaps planning to exchange children with particular needs. For example, two classes might be split between them in order to provide more fully for children with special needs or for more able children or, where there are substantial numbers of children whose home language is not English, for a group to be taught in their mother tongue by a bilingual teacher or assistant.

Planning for a wide range of children

For just a year David had been head of a two-form-entry junior school on the outskirts of a big industrial town. The school attracted a wide variety of children. About 25 per cent were from Asian backgrounds, and the school also drew from both a run-down area of the town and from a middle-class suburban area. There were a number of children with special needs, some with statements, and a few extremely able children. David spent his first year getting to know the staff, talking with them and seeing them teach. He also spent time talking to the children and their parents, did a good deal of teaching himself and got to know each class in the school. Some of his staff were fairly set in their ways, and he realised that the necessary changes would take time.

He was keen to introduce a more personalised approach in order to meet more effectively the wide range of children's needs. He planned an in-service day at the beginning of the autumn term to discuss how they might do more to cater for the range of children. He knew from his observations of the staff that most of them made some attempt to differentiate work according to children's ability and background, and he planned to build on this. He therefore started by asking each teacher to talk about how s/he managed to provide for the wide range of children within his or her class. They discussed this for some time and found this helpful. He then went on to suggest that each teacher should take a school-wide responsibility for a particular group of children, in a similar way to the special educational needs coordinator (SENCO). There would be someone with responsibility for very able children, for children from other cultures (perhaps differentiating between Asian and Afro-Caribbean children), for bilingual children, for the differing performance of boys and girls, for children from disadvantaged homes and for middle-class children. Their responsibility would be to provide the school with information about how each group was doing at regular intervals, perhaps making a regular survey of the performance of the group for which they were responsible so that they could advise colleagues on ways of catering for them and ensure continuity from year to year. This would be rather similar to the roles they already had for subject leadership.

The staff talked this idea through and, while they thought it sounded like a lot of work, they thought the idea had merits and were willing to give it a go.

There are many other areas in which teachers and assistants can profitably share ideas about practice. Discussion about ethos for the whole school and for individual classes is helpful, and teachers can consider what they can do in their classes to support the school ethos and create a learning environment for their children. In particular, a positive approach is helpful in supporting learning, and teachers need to consider how often they make positive or negative comments to children or comments that can be interpreted as negative. This may be a useful thing for an observer to note. A teacher might ask a teaching assistant to note how often s/he makes a positive or negative comment in the course of a class lesson and to whom the comment is made. This will enable the teacher to see whether there are too few positive comments and whether some children get too many negative comments. It will also encourage the assistant to be aware of the importance of making more positive than negative comments.

Teachers and assistants can also consider whether the classroom ethos is one of encouraging children in the view that they can all learn if they really try and seek help when necessary. Do the teacher and assistant encourage children to aim high and show that they have high expectations of them? Are children encouraged to work together and be supportive and helpful to each other? Are they developing good social skills? Are they developing self-awareness, recognising their own strengths and the areas in which they need to develop further? Are they acquiring learning skills and independence in learning? Are they motivated? What is the evidence for this?

Teachers can also share ideas about the rules and routines they use in the classroom and the effect of these on children's development and learning. It is helpful if there is some agreement across the staff about some basic rules, so that teachers do not have to teach children completely new rules when they change classes. On the other hand, different teachers will want to stress slightly different things, and the rules need to change as children grow and develop, so there will always be a place for establishing classroom practice at the beginning of the school year.

It is also helpful to have some agreement about how emotional and social development is to be tackled. What should be done on this at each stage, and what should the school be aiming to achieve? What social skills should be emphasised and discussed with children at each stage? What should teachers and assistants do to help children to manage their feelings and relate well to each other? Such a programme is more likely to be successful if it is taught and emphasised at all stages. It may also be helpful to discuss approaches to social learning.

Questions to think about

1   How can we work together to learn and develop our work with children?
2   What would a class where personalised learning was the norm actually look like?
3   What moves have we already made in this direction?
4   How can we help children to acquire learning skills and become independent learners? What learning skills do they need at different stages?
5   What social skills do we want children to develop? What role do we see for social skills in children's learning in the curriculum?
6   What professional development opportunities do we need in order to make children's learning more personalised? What can I learn from working with a colleague?
7   What can we learn from visiting each other's classrooms?
8   What can we learn from seeing each other teach?
9   What part can teaching assistants and LSAs play in making children's learning more personalised?

Chapter 3

The children

Children develop in many ways through the primary years. Human development tends to be similar for everyone, but the way each individual moves through the stages is extremely variable. Children with special educational needs of different kinds will move through much the same stages of development as other children but often at a much slower rate, and it will be important to recognise the stages they are at in order to provide them with work that is within their capability. Children who are highly intelligent, on the other hand, will move through the stages much more quickly, and this too can cause problems because they may be well ahead of the class in their thinking and need much more demanding work. In some countries children who are exceptionally able are promoted in higher classes. This appears to be successful, but it may cause problems at later stages. It has not been common practice in Britain, but it is worth considering whether a child who is far ahead of his or her contemporaries should perhaps do some work with an older class if this can be arranged. Boys and girls also develop at different rates, with girls usually ahead of boys of the same age during the primary years. Boys may catch up later.

Children's backgrounds

Children who have been to nursery school or playgroup are likely to have developed a number of skills that will be relevant to their later learning. They will have experienced playing with other children, and this will have helped to develop their social skills and use of language as a means of communication. They will have been introduced to books and discussed pictures and have some idea about what the printed word represents. They may be able to recognise their own names. They will have started to count and will have develop ideas about shape, volume and size from their play. In short, they will have developed many of the skills that will form a basis for their later learning.

There will also be some children who have been at home during their early years, and these children may have had more limited experience of playing with others. However, they may have developed good language skills because their parents have talked to them and encouraged them to communicate verbally. Parents may also have read to them and pointed out words, and in some cases a child may have made a start on learning to read. Very intelligent children quite often learn to read before they come to school and will probably need a more personal programme than some of the other children. Parents may also have counted things with their children and talked about money and given them a chance to buy things themselves. Such children may need experience of being with other children, but they will have made a good start on school learning.

There will be other children who will not have experienced so much at home, although the evidence suggests that nearly all parents talk with their children a great deal. There will also be children who have little or no knowledge of spoken or written English, for whom starting school may be quite traumatic. In some cases the experience of being in a foreign land where very little seems to be familiar will add to the children's confusion. Such children need good support from their teacher so that they can learn to trust and become part of their new environment.

Finding out about the children

The staff of a school looking to create more personalised learning need to consider very carefully the way that information about children can be built up, starting with reception – or a nursery class if there is one. The information will come at first from parents, and the teachers of the reception class and the nursery will need to make themselves responsible for finding out all they can about the children coming to them. What do they like doing at home? What do they seem good at? Do they have any feeding problems or likes and dislikes of particular foods? Can they use a knife and fork? Can they manage in the toilet without help? Can they dress themselves? Can they count? Do they enjoy looking at books? Can they recognise their written names or any other words? Do they play with other children? Have they had any illnesses that would affect their work at school? Where many children are of another culture and do not have English as their first language, the school may want to know whether the children have any English and what language they actually speak. These questions will be more difficult to answer where many parents do not speak English, but there may be help from a bilingual teacher or assistant or a parent who can speak English well and who also speaks the language(s) of other parents.

Where children come into the reception class from a nursery or a play group, the school needs to ask similar questions of the staff there as well as asking the parents for information.

This information becomes the starting point for the child's record. The staff as a group need to agree on the records it would be helpful to have for all children. Individual teachers will, of course, want to keep their own particular records, but it is helpful if everyone agrees on recording some specific information, particularly when a child moves from one class to the next. There should be some information that everyone agrees should be contained in each child's record at each stage. Teachers may also find it helpful to share information about the records they keep individually about each child, so that they can learn from each other's practice. The school may offer guidance on this.

Finding out about children in a new class

Molly taught Year 6 in a junior school. As the end of the school year approached she started thinking about the children she would have in her class next term. She talked with Ruth, the Year 5 class teacher, and they decided that Molly should have the opportunity to talk to the children who would be coming to her and ask them to write something about themselves for her. Ruth would take her Year 6 class for a lesson while she did this. Molly told the Year 5 class that she would like to hear whether they had any brothers and sisters, particularly if they were in the school too. She would be interested in what they liked doing in their spare time at home and the things they liked best at school. She would also like to hear about any things they found difficult and the lessons they most enjoyed. It would help her to help them if they could tell her of any work where they felt they needed more help. All this information would be useful to her when she started teaching them in the autumn.

She also spent a good deal of time talking with Ruth. They discussed the children who had special needs and Ruth talked about what she had found seemed to help them most. They also discussed three children who, Ruth said, seemed to be very able. They were capable of working in a very concentrated way and came up with some very original ideas. One of them, John, was an untidy writer but his work was very good when the writing was clear enough to read. She had given him lots of opportunities for writing on the computer, which helped him to produce much more presentable work. One girl, Jill, produced some really good poetry and particularly

continued

liked having a choice of things to write. The remaining child, Tommy, seemed to have technical abilities. He did especially well in technology and also did well in maths and science, and he had lots of ideas about experiments and ways of making things and did a lot of work on these ideas at home. They also talked about the children who could pose behaviour problems and what seemed to work best with them.

Molly was really pleased with all this information. She made copious notes as they talked and was very grateful to Ruth for all her help.

If the children in the new class are reading and writing competently, it is a good idea to give them each a questionnaire asking questions of the kind shown in the Box on p. 13. The replies and any pieces of writing by the children about themselves can then be placed in a loose-leaf file with a section for each child in the class. A further sheet for each child can be used for notes of observations of children made by the teacher or teaching assistant.

The task is somewhat different with the younger classes because you will need to get this kind of information by talking to them, their parents or their former teacher. The teacher's first task with new reception-class children is to discover what stage of development each child is at, and what s/he can already do, in order to build on the child's previous experience. Some of this information will come from parents or from the nursery or playgroup, but you will need to explore further with individual children. This is not an easy task because children of this age are very demanding and there will be only limited opportunities to spend time with an individual child finding out what s/he knows and can do. A teaching assistant can be very valuable here, providing an extra person to observe the children, talk with them individually and help to find out about them. As teacher you need to be clear in your own mind about the information you want to gather about individual children so that you can listen for clues about their existing knowledge and development. This kind of informal observation will give you a good deal of information about each child. You will not only find out what s/he knows and can do but also his or her ideas, temperament and interests and how independent the child has become. You will also find out about the child's personality and social development by observing how s/he interacts with other children. This information will help you when you come to discuss targets with individuals.

You also need to be good at recording what you observe informally and try to note down for your file what you have discovered incidentally in the course of your work with the children. It is particularly useful to note anything that seems to be important in getting to know an individual child, and this may also give you clues about what to do next.

Child development

Children develop in many ways. You will observe physical development as children grow. Language will be developing, and children will be acquiring new words and ways of saying things. They should also be developing socially and be gradually developing skill in working and playing with others. Observing children's play in the early years will tell you a good deal about how an individual child is developing. You will be able to see whether s/he is developing skills in relating to others, learning to take turns, joining in with a group, using language to communicate with others and so on. The classroom environment helps to determine how well the children develop and achieve. The materials you provide for play and learning give rise to social learning and intellectual development, and observation of the way that children use what is available and what they say about it gives clues to the way their thinking is developing.

The work of Piaget (1952), among others, tends to be familiar to primary school teachers and gives us a useful guide to certain stages of development in children. He suggests that human beings have to adapt to their environment in order to survive. The young child acts on the external environment to gain control and in doing so learns the nature of things around him or her. This stage develops further as the baby learns and increases his or her control over the things around. There is further development as the child becomes mobile and explores new aspects of the environment and gradually develops independent thought. Thinking at this stage tends to be egocentric.

Other researchers have suggested that some of his findings do not always hold when a rather different situation is encountered. His research on conservation, for example, was carried out in a rather artificial situation, and when the same experiment is carried out in a more natural one the findings are somewhat different. (McGarrigle and Donaldson 1974; Donaldson 1978). His findings are a useful guide, but you need to make your own judgements of each child's development as well.

By about two years of age the child develops what Piaget terms 'pre-operational thinking', and this stage normally lasts until the child is about six. This is a stage of rapid physical development during which the child becomes fully mobile and an increasingly competent speaker. However, children's judgements are still based on the evidence of their senses, and their thinking is egocentric so they find it difficult to understand what is not present. Eventually, children become what Piaget calls 'concrete operational thinkers', with organised systems of mental activity that allow them to think through a problem, to see it from different points of view and to use previous experience to explain present experience. This stage lasts for most of the primary school years.

The final stage is that of 'formal operations', which children reach as they grow into adolescence. At this stage they can think abstractly. They can theorise about situations and form hypotheses. A few very able children will get to this stage towards the end of primary school, and you need to note this and provide more demanding work that involves more abstract thinking. Such children should be encouraged to work independently, making choices and planning work for themselves.

More recent studies have emphasised the effect of family and community upon the young child. A child learns by interacting with those around him or her as well as exploring the environment. Language is developed in this way, and the experiences and the language to express feelings about what is happening come from interacting with others, first the family and later other children, teachers and adults. Social relationships and social inter-actions determine much of the way children develop. The choices we make and the options open to us are largely influenced by those around us. Children do not always follow the same stages of development because of their different experiences and interactions and the language they learn from these.

There are many other explanations about the way children grow and develop their thinking, and the important thing for the teacher to discover is the way each child is thinking and acting on his or her thoughts. This is not easy. A good deal of information will come out in talking to children, observing them and listening to what they say. Look for children's reactions to different kinds of work and different approaches to learning. Some children are visual learners and learn best when they see pictures or videos. Others learn best when they can be active, either physically or mentally. Another group of children have logical minds and enjoy mathematics and solving problems and puzzles. Boys, in particular, seem to like group work and work where there are clear objectives that can be achieved fairly quickly. These learning styles are not fixed and immutable, and you would be wise to try to interest children in learning in a variety of styles while at the same time acknowledging that some children learn better in particular ways. There is a temptation to assume that children learn in the same way that you do.

There are many clues to children's thinking that you can learn from if you are alert to them. A teaching assistant will also be able to help with this if you explain what you are looking for and encourage him or her to look for information about individual children and tell you about it. Children's errors often give you clues to their thinking, and it is wise to emphasise the idea that making mistakes is part of learning. A child's incorrect answer to a question may alert you to his or her thinking and help you to help the child to think differently. There is evidence that children are often shy of answering questions because they are afraid of making mistakes in front of the class, and so often they are trying to guess what the teacher is thinking. It is helpful to reassure them that you will not be cross about an incorrect answer and would rather they tried to answer the questions than hesitated to put their hands up. One way round this is to direct questions at particular children sometimes.

Language development

During the pre-school years normally developing children acquire language. Hearing others speaking introduces sounds that the child tries to imitate in the sounds s/he produces prior to the development of speech. The parent or carer responds to the child's sounds and reinforces anything that sounds like a word with attention, often repeating it and praising the child for trying. In this way the baby gradually learns a number of words. The next stage is to acquire an understanding of grammar and word order, which allows the child to say whole phrases or sentences. There will be mistakes at this stage where the child applies rules s/he has deduced indiscriminately, such as the occasions when a child says 'I runned round the garden' or 'I goed to see my Granny', but gradually speech develops and most children can talk happily to others by the time they start school. Listening to a child's speech can give the teacher or assistant many clues about how well his or her speech has developed.

There will be some children whose speech is at an earlier stage when they start school, and they will need help with expressing themselves. LSAs will be especially valuable with such children. There may also be some children who are at a very early stage of learning English, but they will have the advantage of having learned another language and will therefore expect equivalent words and rules; although such assumptions will not always be valid, they may help. Bilingual support will be valuable here, and there may be a place for providing opportunities for older children who are speakers of the same home language to talk with new learners of English and help them to understand.

Social development

In watching children play you can learn a good deal about the level of confidence each child possesses and his or her ability to get on with others. You will also learn about some of the skills a child has acquired, the things that seem to interest him or her, the extent to which s/he can pursue a goal and persist in an activity until satisfied with the result. On the more negative side you will see some children who always want their own way, who push others out of the way mentally or physically, who try to dominate others and create an element of conflict. You may need to intervene in such cases, to try to get the child concerned to see other people's points of view, which may be difficult for very young children. Social development is important, and discussion about the need to imagine and think about how someone else is feeling can help. The teacher might tell a story about a child who was verbally attacked by another and ask, 'How do you think that made the first child feel?' At some stage this may be a good topic for discussion in circle time. This is all part of emotional development, and observation of how children react emotionally to different situations will give you an idea of how much control they have over their own feelings.

The self-image

A very important part of any child's growth is the development of the self-image. As teacher you need to find out all you can about how each child sees him or herself. Have parents and others helped them to be positive about their person? Do they believe they are capable people who can learn and do things and get on with other people or do they feel likely to fail and do badly in what they attempt to do? It is important to try to make every child feel positive about themselves, able to do things and learn, and you need to give encouragement to all the children, but particularly any who seem timid and diffident about their abilities. This is especially important for children with learning difficulties. They will quickly come to the conclusion that they are not as clever as some of the other children, and you will need to build up their confidence and praise even very small steps. There are now P levels, which are part of the National Curriculum for children who are working below level one, and you may have some children in your class who would benefit from aiming at these levels and gain confidence from achieving them.

Intelligence

One aspect of knowing children is making judgements about their intelligence. Intelligence is a complex subject. At one time, people thought it was something that you inherited and that was fixed for life. More recently, we have come to see that much can be done to increase a child's inherited intelligence. There have also been recent ideas suggesting that there are many kinds of intelligence. Gardner (1983) suggests that we have a number of types of intelligence. He lists the following: linguistic; musical; logical-mathematical and scientific; bodily kinaesthetic, which includes art and movement; and personal intelligence or ability to get on with other people. These are not fixed forms of intelligence, and we should aim to develop multiple intelligences in all children. They give pointers to possible directions in which you can try to find approaches and tasks that fit different children's particular abilities, celebrating their differences and particular abilities and skills and giving as many children as possible the message that they are good at something.

Emotional intelligence

Goleman (1996) writes of emotional intelligence and suggests that this plays a more important part in life success than intelligence quotient (IQ). He suggests that there are the following aspects of emotional intelligence:

1 Knowing one's own emotions – self-awareness – recognising a feeling *as it happens*.
2 Managing emotion.
3 Motivating oneself.
4 Emotional self-control.
5 Marshalling emotions in the service of a goal.
6 Recognising emotions in others.
7 Handling relationships.

Dealing with emotion

Roger was a problem to his reception class teacher because he frequently became very angry and this often caused conflict with other children. He would strike out when someone did something he disliked and throw work on the floor if he had difficulty

continued

with it. He would swear at others, including Julie, the class teacher, and she was at her wits end about how best to manage his behaviour, which disrupted the whole class.

She talked it over with her teaching assistant, Marion, who was a mother of four children and had had a lot of experience of dealing with children's problems as one of her sons was hyperactive and caused her some difficulty. Marion suggested that when Roger started having a temper tantrum, she would take him out of the classroom so that he did not affect the other children so much. She would take him to somewhere quiet and talk with him about his problems.

Julie thought this was a good idea. Next time Roger gave a display of temper, Marion took him by the hand and led him out of the classroom. When they got to the library she asked him to explain why he was so angry. In talking about it he gradually became calmer. She then talked about how worried about him both she and his teacher were. They wanted to help but he did not make it easy. They talked about the kinds of things that made Roger angry. As they talked, she became aware that his self-esteem was very fragile. He said he got cross when he could not do things or when somebody implied that he was stupid. He felt that he was not as clever as other children and people did not like him.

Marion did her best to reassure him and said that both she and Julie thought he was really intelligent – too intelligent to lose his temper so often. They talked about ways he could try to deal with his anger. She suggested that he should stop himself by thinking of something or someone he really liked. She and Julie would make a chart for him and mark each day he got through without losing his temper. If he got through a whole week, they would put a star on his chart. If he got three stars in three consecutive weeks, Julie would write to his parents to say how well he was doing. He liked this idea and promised to try not to lose his temper so often. She then took him back to the classroom where he got on with his work quietly.

Marion told Julie about their discussion and suggested that they should do all they could to raise his self-esteem, finding occasions to praise and encourage him and tell him that he had abilities. Julie agreed to the chart idea, and they put it into action. His parents, who were worried about his tempers, were very pleased with this idea.

Roger did not improve all that quickly, but there was a slow improvement, and he gradually became more calm and able to keep his temper.

The effect of expectations

For you as teacher, an important aspect of working with children is the expectations you hold for them. You also need to be careful to demonstrate that you have high expectations of them in terms of their progress towards their targets. It is easy to make a comment that suggests that you do not expect much from a child. A comment such as 'That's very good for you' implies that you did not expect much in the first place, and you need to be alert to such slips and try to be positive in dealing with children at the same time as being realistic and showing that you expect a bit more than the child is currently achieving. This is particularly important with children who do not stand out as being difficult or either very bright or very slow (see p. 19: Noting positive and negative comments).

Assessment and evaluation

Many of the ideas put forward in this chapter will contribute to your records of individual children's development and progress. Your observations of children, your study of their work and your discussions with individuals give you information about how much they are understanding and clues about what to do next. An important part of the evaluation

Noting positive and negative comments

There is a case for asking an assistant to note for you, in a lesson that s/he is observing, the positive comments you make and the children to whom you make them, and similarly any negative comments. There will also be some neutral comments. This will alert you to the children who get most and least attention from you and also the extent to which you make positive and negative comments. Do you talk to boys more than to girls? Do you make more negative comments than positive comments to boys or girls? How much attention do the most able children get from you? How much do the least able get?

process is the setting of targets with and, where possible, by the children themselves. These give the children a clear idea of what they are aiming for and give you – and them – criteria for judging how well they are doing. Assessment can take many forms. With younger children you will be assessing how they perform orally and in a limited amount of written work. With older children oral performance will still be important, but exercise books will also give you a good deal of information, and you may also use tests to find out how much individuals know. Listening in when children are working in groups will give you information about how individuals perform when working with others, and discussion with individuals will help you to get a picture of how they are thinking. All this information helps you to build pictures of individuals and to match work to each of them according to their needs.

Questions to think about

1   What stage of development has each of the children in my class reached? What is my evidence for this?
2   What information do I need about the children when I take over a new class? How can I obtain this?
3   What records should I keep of the development and learning of the children in my class? What is the best way of doing this?
4   How can teaching assistants and LSAs contribute to my records?
5   How well are the children in my class developing socially? What is my evidence for this?
6   Have I any children who have poor self-esteem? What can I do about this?
7   What different kinds of intelligence have the children in my class? How can I make use of this information?
8   How can I contribute to children's emotional development?
9   What expectations have I of the children in my class? What do I do to show them that I expect much from them in a way that does not discourage them?

Chapter 4

Learning and teaching

Personalised learning involves matching learning to the individual child. As we saw in Chapter 1, this does not mean teaching each child individually but trying to cater in various ways for the range of children you have in the class. This means knowing the children well and being aware of their different learning styles, aiming within a lesson to provide opportunities for those who learn best by seeing something, those who learn by reading or listening and fitting what they hear into their mental filing system, and those who need to be active to learn.

The learning process

Children start to learn before anyone starts to teach them. They learn through exploring their environment, through play on their own or with others, by imitating parents and older children and by talking with adults and with each other. By the time they go to nursery and later to school, they already know a good deal. This will be extended by their contact with other children and adults and by teaching of various kinds.

The role of experience in learning

When children meet new experiences they look at where they fit in with what they already know. By the time they come to school they already have a good deal of experience of various kinds and the task of a teacher trying to personalise learning is to tap into this experience in order to be in a position to help the child fit new learning into his or her existing knowledge. Effective learning depends upon experience. Memories of experience will be structured in some way in children's minds as they develop concepts and new ideas about the world around them. When they meet a new experience they will try to see how it fits with their previous experience. Telling is only effective if you can link it with experience. In planning learning you need to think of the experiences children will need to understand the new learning. Sometimes you will simply talk about possible relevant experiences and draw out ideas from the children. On other occasions you will want to provide an experience as a starting point for new learning and help children to consider where it fits in with what they already know.

Concept development

You can support the process of turning experiences into concepts by helping children to structure their learning, getting them to think about how things might be grouped and ordered, helping them to remember similar experiences and put new ideas into their minds' filing systems. Science offers many opportunities for tapping into children's experiences. The same will be true in technology. Discussion about a story might include children thinking about experiences they have had that are similar to those of the people in the story, followed by discussion about what they learned from the experience.

Independence in learning

The overall aim is to help children to reach their full potential by becoming independent learners with the skill to decide how best to learn something and to put that skill into practice. This means that acquiring learning skills is a very important part of learning at every stage. There is much to be said for discussing with children how they think they learn best. With older children it may be a good idea to ask them to complete a questionnaire about how they learn. This can include questions giving a choice of ways of learning, for example, listening to the teacher, discussion with a partner or a group, reading, observing something such as an experiment in science, using a computer and anything else you or they can think of. This will give you an idea of how your children see their learning and will provide pointers to ways of helping them learn. With younger children you can ask for a show of hands about their preferences for different ways of learning.

The place of choice

Another aspect of making learning more personalised is to see that there is some choice in what they do. This may be a choice of the order in which they do something or a choice from a number of activities that lead to similar learning. Many of the tasks you ask children to do have a measure of choice within them. For example, writing news or writing a story gives children a choice of what they include. A project will involve a variety of ideas that the children suggest, adding to your ideas about the way the work might proceed. With guidance from you, the children can then choose the ideas that most appeal to them. In some other areas, such as mathematics, it may sometimes be more difficult to offer choice, but there will be opportunities if you look for them. Asking children to find different ways of doing the same calculation gives choice as well as helping children to discover different ways of calculating. Making choices gives an opportunity for the children to make decisions and to think out the way they want to learn. It will also reveal something of the way in which different children think and learn. It can help to provide for the variety in the way children deal with learning tasks and gives the teacher guidance in ways of approaching their learning and trying to match their interests and abilities. You can plan the range of possible activities with these differences in mind.

Learning skills

An important task for the teacher is that of ensuring that children acquire the skills of learning. Discussion about planning work, both as a class with you and with a partner or a small group, can involve speculating, hypothesising, thinking of ideas and discussing them in preparation for individual work. Children need to acquire thinking skills such as reasoning, logical, analytical and creative thinking, problem-solving, seeking and processing information and evaluation. They need to learn the skills of enquiry and questioning and be able to investigate something, asking relevant questions about why and how things happen and how things work, testing out their ideas and drawing conclusions and presenting them.

Investigation and problem-solving

Investigation is an important area of learning. It may involve considering first how to find information and then how to organise it in relation to the topic being considered, perhaps listing things under different headings or making a table or a plan.

Problem-solving and investigation involve using skills of reasoning, being able to predict and anticipate events, using the language of cause and effect and looking for evidence to support reasoning. Older children will need to acquire skills in reading and in making notes from reading and from observation. The ability to use ICT for information, investigation and presentation will be important here, and children need to learn the skills of using it as soon as possible.

Learning through discussion

A good deal of practice in using learning skills can be provided by giving children time to discuss a topic in pairs or small groups. They will need to learn how to use discussion profitably, considering what is involved and how to think about and question what others say. They also need to learn to make counter-proposals and learn from each other.

Mind-maps

Making mind-maps can help the process of structuring ideas. Start by doing this together for a piece of work on a particular topic, drawing the map on the board as you go. This then provides different activities from which children can choose. This is also a good activity for children to undertake in pairs or groups in relation to a particular piece of work, after you have demonstrated how to do it with the class as a whole. It may be a starting point for a piece of writing, and in this case the map needs to be translated into an ordered list of the different aspects of the work to be covered.

Learning through play

Young children learn through play. *Curriculum Guidance for the Foundation Stage* (Department for Education and Skills 2000) suggests that:

> through play, in a secure environment with effective adult support, children can:
>
> - explore, develop and represent learning experiences that help them make sense of the world;
> - practise and build up ideas, concepts and skills;
> - learn how to control impulses and understand the need for rules;
> - be alone, be alongside others or cooperate as they talk or rehearse their feelings;
> - take risks and make mistakes;
> - think creatively and imaginatively;
> - communicate with each other as they investigate or solve problems;
> - express fears or re-live anxious experiences in controlled and safe situations.

This provides a useful guide for assessing the effectiveness of play. Is the children's play providing opportunities for these kinds of learning? What could you introduce to make it more effective?

Social skills and group work

At all levels children need social skills in working with other people. This starts with sharing in play in the nursery and develops as children grow. Children need to learn to listen actively to others and respond to them sensitively, interacting with them as they participate in shared activities. They need to learn about how an action seems from another person's point of view and to reflect on their actions and comments, taking others into account. This is very difficult for young children, but the ability to take another's viewpoint develops as they grow and needs to be encouraged by talking about how people feel in different situations.

At the early stages children need to learn to take turns and share fairly, playing together and learning to recognise the body language of others. The teacher can do much to help the development of this ability by dealing with situations where a child has hurt or upset another by discussing how he or she would feel if s/he were on the receiving end of the action. Circle time is a good opportunity to discuss such issues, and stories can often help, followed by questioning about how the children would feel in similar situations to those in the story. There is a case for discussing body language and how you can tell how someone else is feeling. There is also a need to discuss how best to resolve conflict, and conflict situations need to be considered with individuals and in groups. At the same time children need to be encouraged to state their point of view and respond to the views of others that are different from their own. Children need to be in a group that is sometimes mixed in ability and gender rather than a friendship group. They need the opportunity to be with others from whom they can learn.

Developing group work

Katherine was a newly qualified teacher in her second term of teaching. Her training had made her enthusiastic about group work, and on her final teaching practice she had had a successful experience of getting children to work in groups. However, when she tried to introduce some group work into her Year 4 class it was far from successful. The children were very noisy, which made discussion difficult, and she found that in some cases they were not discussing the topic set but were arguing among themselves and talking about last night's television. Some children did not contribute much and others hogged the limelight by talking most of the time.

She was worried about this and raised the problem with her induction tutor, Megan, who was also a Year 4 class teacher. Megan observed another attempt at group work and made some suggestions. She suggested that Katherine should structure the groups more. In the lesson she had observed, the groups were formed by rearranging the seating of groups of children sitting near together. This meant that quite often groups were formed mainly from boys or mainly from girls. There was also a tendency for friends to be in the same group. Megan suggested that Katherine should select groups so that each had a mixture of girls and boys, able and less able children. This would mean more reorganisation of the classroom but was likely to make discussion more productive.

Katherine tried this and found that while the children did not like it much, the organisation did make a difference.

Megan then suggested it was also important to think about the tasks she was giving to the groups as boys, in particular, as well as some girls, liked practical problems where it was really clear what they were expected to do. For example, groups might discuss how they could set about a study of their school field, which had many different plants and trees growing in it. Or they might consider how they would find out what plants needed for growth by studying the plants that were growing in the classroom and planting seeds to observe their growth. This, too, made for more successful work.

Megan next suggested that she should spend some time with the whole class discussing what made good discussion in groups. Katherine did this, and the children suggested that listening to each other was important as well as making sure that everyone had a chance to say something. She asked them whether it would be a good idea to have a leader in each group. Most of them thought it would be, and they went on to discuss what the role of the leader should be. After a lot of discussion it was agreed that a good leader would see that everyone had a chance to say something and would see that the group kept to the point and came to some conclusions.

Katherine found all these suggestions helpful and her group work gradually became effective.

Paired work and questioning

Sometimes discussion can start in pairs, which then link up into fours or sixes, each pair reporting on their own discussion. It is a good idea when questioning the class to pause after asking a question and suggest that before answering they talk with a partner about the question you have asked. This gives them time for thought and makes questioning much more useful. So often when you ask the class a question, children spend time trying to guess the answer you want rather than thinking about the question.

The Primary Strategy makes a number of points about questioning. It classifies questions as prompting, probing or promoting. Prompting questions are useful when you want to find out how much children already know about the topic you are about to introduce. Probing questions help you to establish the extent of children's knowledge and are particularly useful when you want to recap on previous work before introducing something new. They are particularly useful, too, in the plenary stage of a lesson. Promoting questions are there to stimulate discussion and help children to think about a particular topic when you are about to introduce something new.

Questioning can help to develop children's ability to think, reflect and analyse. It can also help you to assess what they have learned and the success of your teaching.

Dealing with incorrect answers

The way you deal with incorrect answers is also important. Try to make it clear that it is safe to make mistakes because this is how you learn. Try to avoid saying too bluntly that the answer is wrong, asking instead how the child arrived at it and perhaps asking other children what they think. When it is clear to the class that the answer is wrong, it may be possible to say something positive to the child, perhaps praising him or her for having a go and stressing that making mistakes is a way of learning.

Seating

There is also some research evidence that children learn more when they are seated in boy/girl pairs than when seated beside friends. Children may not like this, but after trying it they will usually agree that they learned more than when seated with their friends. Seating is important for children's learning, and sitting beside one's friends is not necessarily the best arrangement, particularly when two children who are slow learners sit together. The opportunity to change around and sit with different people may help learning because children teach each other to some extent, particularly if there are many opportunities for paired or group discussion. They each bring different experiences to their learning and these can be shared.

The effective classroom climate

The climate of the classroom is crucial for the learning process. Hay McBer (2000) in a research report into teacher effectiveness makes the following statement: 'Climate is a measure of the collective perceptions of pupils regarding those dimensions of the classroom environment that have a direct impact on their capacity and motivation to learn.'

The teacher's role

The climate is mainly created by the teacher. Good teachers are enthusiastic, have high expectations and communicate this to the children. They care about children and show this in all their dealings with them. They aim to be as positive as they can in working with children, encouraging them not to be afraid of making mistakes, and they do all they can to help children to develop a positive self-image, especially those children with

Planning for individual children

Mary was deputy head of a junior school and a Year 6 teacher. She was responsible for the performance management of nearly half of the staff and it occurred to her that a similar system for the children in her class could be very helpful. Of course, it would be very time-consuming to interview each child in detail, but it would be possible to do something of this kind.

She decided that a starting point would be to ask the children to write about their work. She gave each child a new exercise book and told them to label it 'My record book'. She wrote a series of headings on the board and asked the children to write their own answers to each heading on the first page. The headings were:

- School work I think I do well
- School work I really like
- School work I find more difficult but would like to improve
- School work I don't much like
- How I learn best
- Some goals for my work this term
- How I will know if I have achieved these goals.

She talked about each heading and explained what she wanted, giving examples of the sorts of goals she would like to see and also information about the ways they could show that they had achieved the goals. She also talked about different ways of learning, such as listening, reading, doing things, working in a group or with a partner, looking at pictures or films or working with a computer.

When everybody had finished, she collected the books in and arranged to see the children individually over a fairly short period of time to discuss what they had written, using times when children were working individually or in groups supervised by her teaching assistant.

She talked over with each child the answers he or she had written down, and she encouraged some children to set more demanding goals and others to be clearer about how they would assess their achievement and when they would do this. She made a point of being very positive with all of them, praising any aspect of their work that she considered good and supporting their ideas for development. At this stage she returned their record books to them.

Towards the end of term, she asked each child to write a report in the record book on what s/he had achieved during the term. At the beginning of the next term she gave them the original task again and saw each child to discuss both his or her report and plans for the new term. She told the children individually what she thought about their work the previous term, and they discussed how far she felt they had achieved their objectives. She made brief notes about the plans and reports so that she had a continuing record of how children were doing. Where a child had written a lot she photocopied the relevant pages.

The plan worked well. The children enjoyed the process, and it helped to make them more independent in their learning and helped Mary to make their learning more individual and better differentiated. She suggested to the head teacher that all classes from Year 4 upwards might be asked to do this. This would enable children to add to their record each year and have a full report on what they had done during the previous four years when they went to secondary school.

special educational needs. Good teachers tell children that they are capable learners and that they believe in their abilities – they make the most of each child's potential. They counter the negative beliefs of some children with praise whenever they can, reframing negative comments more positively, while acknowledging at the same time how the child feels. They never ridicule or use sarcasm with children, and when they need to criticise something they try to find something they can praise to offset the criticism. They make frequent use of praise, particularly relating it to a specific achievement or behaviour by an individual child. The children are made to feel valued and good about themselves, and this results in a readiness to work on task.

The learning environment

The classroom of the effective teacher is well organised: materials are set out in advance, and resources are easily accessible for the children and are arranged so that they can be returned to the right place after use. There is good display, both of children's work and of material to stimulate children. The work displayed is representative of all the children. The material displayed includes a list of the targets the class is currently aiming towards. There are also questions that stimulate thinking, problem-solving and prompt exploration, suggestions for ways of learning things and lists of problem-solving strategies.

Lessons are well prepared, with clear goals shared and discussed with the children. Teaching is often interactive and offers a variety of opportunities to match the needs of all the children. Explanations are clear and work is structured and well presented. There are a variety of approaches to learning, and work is well matched to individual needs. Both the very able and those with special needs have work that takes their abilities into account. Questioning is well handled, with opportunities for children to think about their answers before replying, and discussion involves all the children in some way. Good records are kept of children's progress, and these give the teacher information about the learning needs of individuals. Children also make good use of computers, sometimes working independently and sometimes in pairs, initially learning the skills of computer use and then using the computer to research information and present it. Computer presentation can be particularly useful for very able children who are sometimes untidy writers. You may also either use programmes that you have designed and found useful for children or seek or encourage children to seek programmes or internet sites that would be helpful to individuals or groups (see p. 27: Scaffolding learning).

Motivation for learning

Children learn best when they are motivated. They will be motivated by the teacher's enthusiasm and by his or her recognition of them as individuals who have the ability to achieve. Some, particularly boys, will be motivated by competition, but this can be demotivating for others and needs to be used carefully. Some boys – and also some girls – will be motivated by computer use, and this can play an important part in personalising learning. They will be motivated too by their own achievement, and the kind of work with individuals suggested in the case study earlier in this chapter is likely to be motivating, especially as it is partly planned by the children themselves setting their own goals. The display of a child's work is likely to motivate, and it is particularly important to see that all children get their work displayed on occasion. Praise and encouragement is motivating and will be particularly important for children with low self-esteem. Try to see that every child gets some praise from you at fairly frequent intervals. Encourage an element of risk-taking, encouraging the view that you learn from your mistakes, although,

Scaffolding learning

Vygotsky (1978) writes of 'scaffolding' children's learning. By this he means providing the support needed when an individual is learning something new. For example, Jean, a Year 1 teacher, was introducing her children to the three-times table by getting them to set out counters in threes to see what each set of counters added up to. In going round the class she discovered that some children counted from one each time they set out the counters. She suggested to them that they should count on from the previous total each time, thus saving themselves some counting. This would be a form of scaffolding.

Margaret, a Year 5 teacher, was planning a topic on weather with her children. They had set up a weather station, monitoring temperature, wind direction, cloud formation and amounts of rain, and they recorded the weather each day. They talked about the possible conclusions they could draw from their records. They found this difficult, and Margaret suggested that they should look for patterns of weather and the things that were present when the records showed particular kinds of weather. What sorts of clouds were in the sky when the weather was windy? What direction was the wind coming from when there was a storm? What did the sky look like when it was very wet?

of course, this needs to be balanced so that children do not think that anything goes. Much depends on the individual child. More confident children can take risks sometimes and can accept that they will sometimes be wrong. Less confident children will need encouragement to take risks because being wrong is damaging to their self-esteem.

You need to think about the motivation offered by extrinsic and intrinsic rewards. Extrinsic rewards are things such as stars, prizes and positive comments about work. Intrinsic rewards are rewards that come about from real interest in the work itself. Intrinsic rewards are more lasting and are something to aim for. However, not all work will inspire all children, and children with low self-esteem can be encouraged with the right sorts of extrinsic rewards, particularly encouragement and praise from the teacher.

Classroom behaviour

In the effective classroom, behaviour is under the teacher's control. There are well-understood classroom rules, based on the school's discipline policy, and children generally keep to them, only occasionally giving the teacher cause to draw upon the school's system of sanctions. Much more often the teacher uses the school's system of rewards and also rewards children with praise for good work and good behaviour.

Questions to think about

1   What experiences do I offer my children to help them learn?
2   How well do I help children to structure work and link it to experience so that they remember it and develop concepts?
3   What am I doing to help children to become independent learners?
4   What part does choice play in the work I do with my children?
5   How much do I know about the learning styles of the children in my class?

continued

6   What learning skills are my children developing? What am I doing to develop their learning skills further?

7   Are my children learning to make good use of ICT both for investigation and presentation?

8   What social skills are my children developing? What further skills do they need to develop?

9   How effective is group and paired work in my class? How effective is class discussion?

10   How do I set about matching work to individuals? Would discussion with each individual child about his or her work be helpful?

11   Am I making effective use of display in my classroom?

12   What sort of a climate is there in my classroom? Do I demonstrate enthusiasm and encourage children enough?

13   How are my children best motivated?

14   Is the children's behaviour in the classroom conducive to good learning?

Chapter 5

Providing for boys and girls

Almost all primary school classes contain both boys and girls. They frequently have very different attitudes to school from each other and to learning, and you need to take their different stances into account in planning for them.

Gender behaviour is socially constructed. Boys and girls learn from their parents and others how to behave appropriately as males or females; their peer group reinforces this, and it is extremely difficult to ignore the pressure towards particular behaviours. By the time children start school they are already 'doing gender'.

Recent years have seen increasing concern about the gap in performance between boys and girls. General Certificate of Secondary Education (GCSE) results have shown increasing differences in performance year by year. Although both boys and girls have improved their performance each year, the gap has increased. It mainly concerns performance in reading and literacy, where girls consistently outperform boys, and they often equal or almost equal boys in mathematics and science. This difference is already present in the infant school. This is a problem not only in this country but also in many other countries. In fact, we tend to do rather better than many other countries, but the problem is still a matter for concern.

Boys often pose problems in class. They may be disruptive, aggressive, inattentive and generally a headache for the teacher as well as preventing the girls from learning. This is not to suggest that all boys perform badly and misbehave. There are studious boys who work well and do as well, if not better, than the girls. Nor does it mean that all girls are conscientious workers for there are some who underperform and create problems. It is important to monitor the performance of boys and girls so that you can remain aware of such differences. It is also important to ensure that girls are not neglected because boys are more demanding and tend to underperform.

Boys' performance needs to be considered alongside ethnicity and social background. Levels of achievement are more strongly influenced by social class and ethnic background than by gender. Some black Caribbean and black African children, particularly boys, tend to be behind their peers from reception onwards. Pakistani and Bangladeshi children also perform badly, although girls still outperform boys. Working-class children, particularly boys, tend to underperform, although here again there are exceptions. The number of boys achieving five GCSEs at grades A* to C per hundred girls decreases as you go down the social scale.

It is very easy for teachers to stereotype children and to expect poor performance from these groups, and this tends to produce just that. Research evidence suggests that some teachers attribute poor performance by boys to lack of effort and poor performance by girls to lack of ability. While this may be true in some cases, it is a somewhat sweeping generalisation.

Reasons for the gender gap

Many reasons have been given for the gender gap. Boys in today's schools may not have a father as a role model at home. The role of men as providers for their families has changed since many more women now work outside the home and work in the home is more often shared. In recent years male sense of purpose and identity has been eroded to some extent, as women now expect to have a career as well as a family.

The effect of testosterone in boys may be to increase aggressive behaviour, which in turn leads to increased testosterone levels. There are few male teachers in primary schools, and the curriculum perhaps does not sufficiently reflect boys' interests. Boys, particularly working-class boys, may have a view of masculinity that conflicts with the kind of behaviour required in the classroom. This view of masculinity sees strength and physical ability as important for males, and playground games for boys very often include violence in some form.

Aspirations for working-class boys tend to be for manual work such as building, plumbing, decorating and so on. Their upbringing will reflect the views of their parents, who may see little value on school education, and peer pressure may lead to a rebellious attitude to authority, valuing physical strength, boisterousness and daring. They may take the view that it is not 'cool' to be conformist and hard-working in school, and older boys may have an 'anti-swot' culture even in the primary school. Academically successful boys may not be popular with their peers. This may not be true of middle-class boys, who are likely to be more competitive and want to outperform their peers.

Girls, on the other hand, tend to be more conformist and enjoy school more than boys. They tend to work harder even when the teaching is not very good. In particular, they enjoy reading and writing, and they do well in these subjects, which has an effect on work in other subjects. Girls are often less confident and less assertive than boys and need more encouragement to play a full part in classroom work.

The differences are apparent even in the nursery, where boys and girls normally choose different activities from each other. Studies have shown that while both boys and girls (when alone or with others of the same sex) may choose to play with the opposite gender toys, when a member of the opposite sex comes along they revert to the gender-appropriate toys. Boys and girls in primary school tend to be attracted to others of the same gender and police others in order to get them to conform to this practice.

Learning preferences

Children tend to have learning preferences, some of which apply to both boys and girls and some of which apply only to one or the other. Girls tend to prefer a quiet, orderly classroom and dislike it when boys disrupt the lesson. Many girls respond well to opportunities to write in a personal way. Boys like to be active, they like practical work, and challenge and discussion in groups or pairs. They are competitive and like activities such as quizzes, where there is the possibility of winning. They are often happy to take risks, which is probably why there are often more boys than girls putting up their hands in answer to a question or to contribute to discussion. They like to have structured lessons with clear objectives and a straightforward route towards achieving them. They enjoy ICT, videos, films and slides. Variety is important for them. Many dislike writing and reading, and their work is often untidy. Learning styles are about emotions and values as well as cognition. Learners bring their personal histories to learning, and these affect their reactions to learning material. They add to their histories as they grow, and their self-images and their attitudes to their learning affect what they can take from it. A child who has often experienced success will be more ready to learn something new, whereas a child who has often experienced failure tends to develop negative attitudes to learning. It is important to show children that you have high expectations for everyone, to combat negative thinking with more positive approaches and to challenge forms of masculinity that work against learning. These lie at the heart of boys' poorer performance, particularly for working-class boys. Middle-class boys tend to have a view of masculinity that values achievement more. Young people choose their learning styles, and boys, in particular, are constrained by social relationships with their peers.

It is important for both boys and girls to cater for a variety of learning styles. These are not fixed and children can change their preferred learning style as they grow and it is important to give both boys and girls opportunities to learn in various different ways, so that they begin to know their own preferences. This is where opportunities for choice are useful, since you can often see children's preferences from the choices they make. You can also gain information about this from the kind of review activities suggested in the last chapter. It is useful to ask children to tell you how they think they learn best. This gives you clues to their learning styles that you can use in planning work.

Teacher behaviour

Miranda was the class teacher of a Year 3 class. She was concerned about the poor performance of some of the boys in her class who appeared to be quite intelligent in discussion but turned in very poor work, even in mathematics and science, where some other boys did quite well, although not much better than the girls. She looked for books in the library that dealt with differences between boys and girls and found that this was a concern for many teachers. One author said that teachers tended to treat boys and girls differently and in class were more likely to ask boys to answer questions than girls.

Miranda thought about this and decided that she would ask Jenny, her teaching assistant, to help her check this out. Jenny would record during a questioning session how many boys and how many girls put up their hands to answer questions and note which boys and girls Miranda chose to answer.

Jenny had been doing her own reading of a book for teaching assistants that stressed the value of observing how the teacher dealt with the children and particularly how he or she talked to them. Without telling Miranda, she decided that she would also record how Miranda responded to each child's answer.

The result was interesting. Boys were much more likely to put their hands up than girls and were also more likely to be given the chance to answer, even though Miranda was very conscious of trying to give equal opportunities to both boys and girls.

The notes of the teacher's responses to children were interesting. She made very encouraging remarks to those who gave acceptable answers, but she was quite dismissive of those who gave wrong or unlikely answers, saying things such as 'I don't know what you were doing when we talked about this' and 'That's a ridiculous answer. Think again.'

Jenny reported on what she had observed and, with some trepidation, gave Miranda the list of her responses to children. Miranda was rather horrified by this and resolved to do something about it.

She thought first about how she could encourage more girls to answer. The books she had been reading suggested that children were sometimes hesitant about putting up their hands in case they gave a wrong answer in front of the class. She then thought about how she dealt with wrong answers and concluded that she needed to be more careful about this. She talked to the class about the fact that you learned from mistakes and said that there was nothing wrong in giving a wrong answer sometimes.

She thought about the kinds of things she could say in response to a wrong answer. She might say something like 'That's interesting – how do you get that answer?' or 'Well tried – that isn't quite right but it is nearly there.' She also gave the children a few minutes to talk in pairs about the questions before asking them to answer.

She found that after a few sessions of dealing better with wrong answers and giving the children time to discuss the answers, more girls were putting up their hands and the answers were better because they had had time to talk and think about the question.

Teacher effects

Every teacher has a personal view of what it is like to teach boys and girls. There is also a temptation to expect poorer work from boys, which is a recipe for getting poorer work from them. Keep your expectations high for both boys and girls and make sure that they are aware that you expect a lot from them. Give them responsibilities and show that you have confidence in them. Asking boys to teach somebody else in the class or even making arrangements for boys to listen to younger children reading can often stimulate them to better concentration.

The fact that boys are likely to be more disruptive than girls leads teachers to pay more attention to the boys. They are more outspoken and assertive, more likely to call out, often openly disparaging of girls. The consequence of this is that teachers tend to pay more attention to boys than to girls, even though they do not intend to do this. There is often a tendency to choose topics and materials with the boys in mind. Boys also take up more space than girls. They move about the classroom more, waste time and disrupt the learning of girls and the more studious boys. There can be a hidden curriculum effect of making girls feel they are less valuable than boys.

Ways of helping boys – and girls – to achieve more

Because boys usually pose more problems than girls and tend to be more demanding, it is easy to arrange things to suit the needs of boys and to take it for granted that girls will fit in. Many of the techniques for improving the performance of boys will also help girls, but girls also need consideration in their own right. Boys quite often demand more of the teacher's attention and tend to corner equipment such as computers to the disadvantage of the girls. They are also inclined, when they can, to leave girls to do the clearing up. As the case study above suggests, they are usually more ready to answer questions and take part in discussion. It is important to see that you give the girls a fair share of your attention, even though this is not always easy to do.

Both sexes like a well-ordered classroom, although many boys and some girls may be good at reducing order to chaos. Both boys and girls like clear explanations and clear lesson aims, and well-structured lessons suit both groups. Oral work is very important, and care must be taken to ensure that both sexes contribute. Boys in particular feel confident when there is good use of visual stimuli, ICT, video and drama. Both boys and girls enjoy group and paired work. The formation of groups is important. It is often a good idea to have roughly equal numbers of boys and girls in a group as well as a mixture of children of different abilities. This provides better opportunities for children to learn from each other, provided the boys give the girls a chance to contribute. Friendship groups tend to have less potential for learning than mixed groups, and it is a good idea to decide on group membership, thinking about how the children can learn from each other. It is important to consider carefully the needs of children who are quiet and to place them in a group where they will feel comfortable about contributing.

Boys and girls have different attitudes to reading and like different kinds of books. If you teach from Year 3 or 4 onwards, you need to do all you can to encourage reading. Boys often prefer factual books to fiction, while girls tend to enjoy stories more. It is a good idea to look at how boys and girls, and men and women, are represented in the fiction books you have available. Do the authors represent boys as the leaders and girls as the followers? You need to see that there are some stories that give girls a leading role and include women as achievers.

You need to do all you can to help boys to become readers, perhaps talking about how a fiction book begins and then leaving the children to find out what happens by reading the book for themselves. Get children to keep an individual reading record of the books they have read, and talk to them individually about what they thought of a particular book. Get boys, in particular, but also girls, to talk to the class about a book they have read and enjoyed. Have a notice-board on which children can post accounts of books they have enjoyed and can recommend to other children, and encourage boys to contribute to this.

Boys and girls tend to show some differences in speech and language use. Girls often have a larger vocabulary, and boys are more inclined to use slang. Girls are more likely to use standard English, and boys – particularly working-class boys – tend to associate working-class speech with masculinity. In spite of popular belief, studies show that men tend to talk more than women. With older children there can be some discussion about language and what is appropriate in various situations. Children can be encouraged to think about how they would say something to a friend of the same sex, to their parents and to their head teacher and to consider the differences. Drama in which children take on the parts of people who normally speak well may help. Drama is a very valuable activity for developing oral language.

Learning by tutoring

Joy was the class teacher of a Year 6 class. She was concerned that her children, particularly the boys, were not very interested in reading. Few of them seemed to read for pleasure and only a small number read for information. She tried various ways to stir their interest, but none of them was very successful.

She came to work sharing a car with Elsa, who was the class teacher of a Year 3 class. They spent a lot of time talking about work and discussed Joy's concern about reading. Elsa felt that the children in her class, too, were not very interested in reading, particularly the boys, and between them they thought up the idea of some of Joy's children hearing some of Elsa's children read. This would help the Year 3 children and would be good for the self-esteem of the Year 6 children. Joy could stress to her class that she wanted them to try to get the Year 3 children interested in reading.

Joy talked to her class about the idea and suggested that four girls and four boys should spend half an hour each afternoon for a fortnight hearing four boys and four girls in the younger class read. In the following fortnight a different set of children would take part and so on. She said she would ask the children who were good readers first because it was important that they gave the Year 3 children a good example. She discussed with them what to do when hearing someone read, what to do if a child could not read a word, and the need to sound encouraging even if a child did not read very well. She also stressed that she and Elsa wanted to get the children of the other class really interested in reading so that they read for pleasure and for information, so it might be a good idea sometimes to talk about books and how interesting reading could be. The children acting as tutors should try to encourage them to read. For that half hour while the tutoring was taking place, the other children in both classes would read independently.

All the children were enthusiastic about this idea and they started to put it into practice. After the first fortnight Elsa reported that the children who had been tutored were disappointed that it had come to the end. They liked their Year 6 tutors and wanted to go on with them. They said they had learned a lot, and more books were borrowed from the class library than previously. The Year 6 children had also enjoyed themselves, and others were looking forward to taking their turn to be tutors. The need for them to be good readers to be tutors encouraged their own reading.

Joy felt that the exercise had helped to bring home to the children the importance of reading and that there was a noticeable rise in interest on which she could build.

Assessment

It was suggested earlier – in Chapter 4 – that there should be careful assessment of the progress of boys and girls, looking at their performance and getting them to assess themselves. There is also a place for pairs of children assessing each other's work. The criteria to be used in self- and peer-assessment should be discussed, and the children should be encouraged to judge each other's work in the light of these criteria. This also makes children very conscious of the need to judge their own work according to such criteria.

The curriculum

The National Curriculum lays down what should be studied, but the children themselves have views about what is appropriate for boys and for girls, and this affects the degree of effort they are prepared to put in and the results that they achieve. Boys tend to feel that science and technology are boys' subjects and language studies are girls' subjects. At a later stage in the secondary school these sorts of views affect their choice of subjects as well as their performance in them, and this in turn affects their career choices. Few students choose careers in what are seen as opposite-sex subjects. Few boys choose to work in child care or nursing and few girls opt for engineering or plumbing.

Questions to think about

1 What differences of performance and behaviour have I noticed in the boys and girls in my class?
2 Do I give more attention to boys than to girls?
3 When I ask a question, do more boys than girls put up their hands? Do I give boys more opportunities to answer questions than girls?
4 Is there evidence of an anti-swot culture in my class? Are boys who do well less popular with others?
5 What subjects and activities do boys like best and least? What do the girls like best and least?
6 What learning styles do the girls and boys in my class appear to have?
7 How do I deal with incorrect or inappropriate verbal responses from children?
8 What expectations do I have for boys and girls? Do I communicate the fact that my expectations are high for everyone?
9 How do I group children for collaborative work?
10 What can I do to encourage children to read?
11 Do the girls and boys in my class use language differently?

Chapter 6

Children with special educational needs

Schools now have a legal responsibility to identify, assess and make provision for children with disabilities. They also have a duty not to discriminate against such children in any way. All children have a right to a broad and well-balanced education. A disability can be defined as an inability to perform as well as other children of the same age in some area of school learning, which may be physical, cognitive or sensory.

Inclusion and integration

Recent years have seen a move towards including as many children with special educational needs as possible in mainstream education, rather than in special schools. This makes considerable demands on teachers but the move has been successful in many cases, giving disabled children a chance to mix and work with other children and learn from them as well as from teachers and LSAs. Some children with disabilities may have difficulty in making friends and communicating with others, and fostering relationships and communication will be an important task for you. It will be important to find out all you can about the particular problems of children with special educational needs so that you are in a strong position to help them. There is also the danger that they will lose self-esteem because they see that they are less able than others. You will need to give them a great deal of encouragement to avoid this happening to a damaging extent.

The success of inclusion depends on the way teaching is organised and the provision made for individuals. However, inclusion is not the same as integration. Integration suggests that the child with special educational needs plays as full a part as possible in the work of the class, whereas inclusion could mean a special educational needs unit in a mainstream school, perhaps making separate provision for these children. Integration means that when the class is studying a particular topic, the child with special educational needs also works on the same topic at his or her own level and is included in the work of the class, often with help from an LSA. The extent to which integration is possible depends to some extent on the severity of the child's disability and the degree of support available in the classroom. Thomas *et al.* (1998) states:

> The principles embodied in inclusion are concerned with a philosophy of acceptance and providing a framework within which all children – regardless of ability, gender, language or cultural origin – can be valued equally, treated with respect and provided with equal opportunities at school.
>
> (p. 82)

They go on to describe ways in which teachers have addressed the problem of providing for a wide range of children, including:

- altering the format of the lesson;
- changing the arrangement of groups;

- changing the ways instruction is delivered;
- using different materials;
- providing alternative tasks (differentiation by activity).

(p. 193)

Schools may choose to deal with the problem of a wide range of ability by grouping or setting and in some cases by withdrawing some children to work with an LSA. These arrangements each have advantages and disadvantages. The advantages are that groups for the less able tend to be kept small and bottom sets may be taught by the SENCO. It allows more able children to work at a higher level and stimulate each other. It also makes it easier for the teacher, since he or she then has a smaller range of ability to deal with and is able to have higher expectations for the children.

The disadvantages are that, however the school tries to disguise the fact that some groups contain lower-ability children, the children in the lower groups or sets are nearly always aware that they are less able, and this is demotivating and damaging to their self-esteem. Lower-ability groups tend to contain more boys than girls and more children from disadvantaged homes. These children also lack the stimulus of good role models – which could come from working with more able children.

This is a problem that nearly every school has to find a way of solving. Probably the best solution is to have some whole-class work, some work that is ability grouped and some work in mixed-ability groups.

The process of integrating children with special educational needs depends to a considerable extent on help from LSAs and other teaching assistants, who are able to work with individual children to enable them to join in with the work of the class to whatever extent is possible.

Integration and inclusion also involve helping children with disabilities to relate to other children, making friends and communicating with them. Initially it may help to develop a 'buddy' system in which a child making normal progress is asked to befriend a child with special educational needs and see that s/he has a chance to join in with other children at playtime and in class where appropriate.

The inclusion of children with serious disabilities makes considerable demands on class teachers, and it is important that help for such teachers is available, perhaps from the school SENCO or from a specialist teacher with expertise with children in the areas of disability that are present in the class. Where a mainstream school has received children from a special school that has closed, there may be members of the special school staff who have transferred to the mainstream school and who will be able to support class teachers. There may also be a need to cooperate with other professionals, such as physiotherapists, psychologists or speech therapists.

Not all schools will have a wide range of children with special educational needs. Some will have a few with learning difficulties and perhaps one or two with physical disabilities or poor sight or hearing. Some will have statements of special educational needs, and others will simply be slower than their classmates.

Self-image and self-esteem

Whatever the range of a child's problems, an important task will be to maintain his or her self-esteem. Every child with a disability will be aware that other children can do things that s/he cannot, and this is depressing for the child concerned and likely to make him or her hesitant about trying anything new. The child's family will have played a part here. They may have been hesitant about letting their child try anything new or they may have been discouraging about what the child does and impatient with his or her slow progress. On the other hand, they may have been encouraging, and they may have praised and supported the child for any attempt to do something new. The parents' attitudes to the child will already have formed her or his self-image in the pre-school years, and the

Learning tables

Pamela was class teacher of a Year 4 class that contained a number of children with special educational needs. Only one of them actually had a statement, but there were several who found learning difficult. Among these were four girls – Selena, Beryl, Gillian and Julie – who had problems with mathematics. Pamela talked to each of them individually and agreed a target with all of them that they would learn their two to five times tables in the next five weeks, giving a week for each table and time at the end for checking whether they had achieved their target. Each girl had a special record book in which they had written their targets with the date by which they had to be achieved. Pamela would sign their books when they had achieved them.

Lucy was the teaching assistant who worked with this class, and Pamela asked her to work with this group each morning, as part of the numeracy hour, helping them to achieve this target. She went through each table in turn, with the girls practising the numbers. When she felt that most of them knew a table, she played a game of Ludo with them, in which they had to answer a table question before they could make each move. If they could not answer, they could not move. They really enjoyed this game, and it gave a lot of practice in the table facts. When Lucy felt they had really learned one table, she moved on to the next table, and when they knew it sufficiently well, they played again, this time having to answer questions from both tables before they could move. Eventually they really knew all four tables, and Pamela gave them a test, which they all passed, so she could sign in their record books that they really knew tables two to five.

school may find a child who is nervous about trying anything and convinced s/he will not succeed or, conversely, a child who believes in him- or herself and is able to make progress. Self-esteem affects motivation, and you need to do all you can to find ways of motivating such children. Tilstone and Layton (2004) note that: 'Individuals build up their identity through the practical processes involved in social interaction, adopting and acting out the "self" they see reflected in the way other people regard them' (p. 170). You need to set an example to the other children of being encouraging about contributions from the children with special educational needs and encourage their peers to act similarly. The important thing to get across is that everyone is of value and should be treated with respect.

It will be important to help children with special educational needs to see their own progress by setting targets with them that they can actually reach. These might be learning or behaviour targets, but as teacher you will need to be encouraging about progress towards them and discourage comparison with more able children. You also need to be careful to demonstrate that you have high expectations of them in terms of their progress towards their targets. Be very careful to avoid giving the impression that you do not expect much. In a class where several children have similar levels of difficulty or similar problems, a little competition with children of similar ability is acceptable, and such children may be encouraged to work together. You also need to look for areas in which their progress is fairly normal and give them opportunities to work in groups with more able children from time to time, so that they have the opportunity to learn from them.

Bullying

Some children with special educational needs may be the victims of bullying. Children who are very different from their peers, perhaps deformed in some way or finding it difficult to relate to others, are particularly likely to suffer in this way, and you need to be alert to this possibility and ready to investigate any complaints, perhaps asking other children to be ready to report any bullying they see. It will be important to stress the need to help such children and befriend them, even when they do not respond easily. It is also important to address the problem as affecting all children and not to do it in such a way that children with special educational needs feel singled out.

Whenever you meet a case of bullying it is important to treat it seriously and try to paint a picture of how the child being bullied felt. When you feel you have got the child responsible for the bullying to understand this, ask him or her to think how s/he could make the bullied child feel better. Is there something nice that the bully could do for him or her?

Learning support assistants (LSAs)

LSAs are appointed to support the needs of particular children and to enable them to join in with the work of the class at a level that they can manage. The SENCO and class teachers need to decide whether support should be restricted to the children with special educational needs or whether other children might also be helped, so that the children for whom the LSA was appointed do not feel singled out too much. It will be also necessary to decide whether children with special educational needs should sometimes be withdrawn from the classroom for work with the LSA or whether all support should be classroom-based. Much depends on the level of each child's needs. It will be important for the LSA to work closely with the class teacher as well as with the SENCO. There will be a need for careful two-way briefing by class teachers and LSAs; the planning work will need to be shared, and the relevant records and findings must be available to both teachers and LSAs. There should be trust between them. Class teachers and LSAs will also need briefing by the SENCO, who can give information about each child with special educational needs and talk over what might help his or her progress.

LSAs will need training and this will be partly a responsibility for the SENCO, but there is likely to be some training externally to help people in these posts. LSAs will need to know something about the National Curriculum and the need to look at all aspects of a particular child's problems. They will also need to know of various approaches suitable for children with different handicaps. There may be some help from teaching assistants, parents or other volunteers, which will ease the lot of the class teacher in providing some individual help, but this will also mean further briefing and explaining what needs to be done and how to approach it.

Social development and communication

We saw earlier that a child with special educational needs may well have a poor self-image, particularly if his or her problems are physical and clearly evident to other children. This may make such children hesitant about forming relationships with others. They may also find communication difficult, and other children may reject their advances. All of this means that they may have difficulty in finding friends, which will reinforce their already poor self-image, and therefore means that they have fewer chances of learning from other children. As teacher you need to work at encouraging other children to include special educational needs children in their activities. The 'buddy' system suggested above may be helpful. It may also be useful to include such children in working groups and encourage the group to give the child with special educational needs opportunities to contribute. It helps to talk to the class about the need to see that at play-time no one is left out, perhaps appointing two or three children to look out for children on the periphery and draw them in. This will be particularly important for autistic children.

Dealing with autism

Jack was autistic. He had been slow to develop language and tended to use it inappropriately. He had difficulty in relating to others, partly because of poor communication skills and partly because his odd behaviour. He tended to be obsessive about particular activities. He was very sensitive to sound and found the classroom buzz when children were working together very disturbing. He was also sensitive to touch, enjoyed stroking things, but did not like being touched by others. He did not make eye contact easily and found it difficult to read other people's body language, and this was disconcerting. He used repetitive phrases that seemed to have no point, but he just liked saying them. He also lacked sensitivity to how others were feeling. He worked best when the programme was carefully structured because he found change and any deviation from the expected threatening.

His class teacher, Hilary, tried hard to help him but it was not easy. She encouraged other children to make approaches to him and try to relate to him as a friend, not giving up when he did not respond, explaining that he had problems and could not help being unresponsive. Edna, the LSA who worked with him, was careful to try to structure things for him so that he could predict what was going to happen next. She also made a lot of use of visual aids, such as a timetable of what he would be doing during a morning or afternoon and an egg timer so that he could judge when the next activity was due to take place.

One activity Edna devised that Jack found helpful was the telling of made-up stories about situations that he found difficult. For example, he did not know how to respond when other children tried to get him to join in as the teacher had asked them to do. Each story introduced the sort of unspoken rules and behaviour that Jack found difficult to understand. Each story also described the way other people felt about a particular situation, such as the reaction of other children who had tried to befriend him when he did not respond in an equally friendly way. This was something to which he was not very sensitive. Such stories gave Edna the chance to discuss such situations with Jack and suggest new ways of behaving so that he became more socially adept. She also tried to introduce information about body language, which he found difficult to read. Progress was slow, but gradually Jack became a little more socially competent.

Assessment and evaluation

Assessment plays an important role with all children with special educational needs and particularly with those whose problems are serious. The *Special Educational Needs Code of Practice* (Department for Education and Skills 2001) lays down a series of actions that a school should take if a child shows that s/he has difficulty with the learning that other children of a similar age manage easily. The process involves initial assessment and provision by the school, usually with advice from the SENCO, then perhaps some specialist help and finally assessment by the local education authority (LEA), which can result in a Statement of Special Educational Needs, which lays down what should be provided, the support needed and the reviews that will be made. At this stage the appointment of an LSA may be recommended. At all stages the parents should be involved, and if it is an older child who is being assessed, s/he should also be consulted. The next task is to make an Individual Learning Plan (ILP) for the child, which sets out the learning that the child should attempt. There will then be regular checks on progress.

There will, of course, be many other children with special educational needs that are not sufficiently serious to warrant a Statement but who nevertheless require individual help, and these children too will need personal programmes, carefully considered targets and regular reviews of progress. LSAs, as well as teaching assistants, may also help with these children, with the school SENCO and the class teacher advising on ways of doing this.

There is now scope in National Curriculum levels of achievement for children who are experiencing considerable difficulty in achieving level 1 to work through P levels, which are a series of steps leading up to level 1.

It will be important for teachers to make regular assessments of all children's progress and to record these, but assessment is particularly important for children with special educational needs. Ofsted (2004), in a survey of provision for children with special educational needs, found that moderation of teacher assessments, while satisfactory in most schools for most children, tended to be less satisfactory for children with special educational needs.

Part of the task of assessment involves target-setting, and appropriate targets need to be set for all children. This means considering children with special educational needs carefully and agreeing appropriate targets with them. Targets should be precise, clearly stated and time-linked so that children know not only what their own targets are but also when they should be reached. Progress towards targets should be reviewed regularly so that children remain conscious of what has to be done and by what date. Children should have somewhere to record their targets and the progress they are making towards them. The record books suggested in Chapter 4 would be useful here. These provide a point of reference and a record of progress. While targets for special educational needs children need to be individual, targets for children progressing normally may be shared among a group of similar ability, but you need to find time to discuss progress towards them on a regular basis, perhaps using the process described in the case study in Chapter 4. With younger children you may need to keep the records and talk them over with individual children regularly.

Room management and the environment

As teacher you need to agree the activities you plan with any supporting staff and to organise the environment so that materials are easily available to the children. You also need to make arrangements for seeing that equipment is returned intact to the correct place. This means training children in good habits and checking that these are followed. One way of doing this is to make one or two children responsible for each small area where equipment and materials are stored. Label the places for each piece of equipment and provide time at the end of each session for returning everything to its correct place and for the children responsible for each storage space to check that everything is there. They should also be responsible for telling you if anything is damaged or broken. It helps to colour code equipment and materials according to where they belong and their purpose and to label the storage spaces with the names of the children responsible for them.

You may also have children in the class who need special pieces of assistive equipment. Some of these, such as hearing aids or glasses, will be the personal property and responsibility of the child although you may have to check that the child is wearing the glasses or the hearing aid and that the hearing aid is turned on and correctly adjusted. Children with physical difficulties may need sticks, frames or wheelchairs and positioning devices to provide them with a seat comfortable for writing. Others may need electronic aids of various kinds. Physiotherapists will be able to advise you on this. Children with poor vision may, in addition to glasses, need large-print material. You need to be continually looking for alternative routes to learning.

Specific disabilities

You may have a number of children with particular special educational needs in your class, some of whom may be withdrawn for specific work to match their particular needs.

You need to know something about each child's needs even if your work is complemented by work with specialists, and you need to learn all you can from specialist staff about particular disabilities. Whatever the disability it is essential to show the children in question that they are valued and can make progress.

Cognitive problems

Many children with special educational needs are those who have difficulty in learning, perhaps caused by developmental delay, perhaps by low intelligence, perhaps by other disabilities and perhaps because of missing school through illness. Whatever the cause, you have the task of finding ways of helping each child to learn. You need first to try to assess the cause of the difficulty and then assess what the child can actually do and understand. If the child has a Statement identifying some of this information, a good deal of assessment will have been done for you. There may also be information from the previous teacher or, if you teach reception children, from the parents or nursery staff. The SENCO may have helpful information, which should be in the child's record.

Your task with the children with the most serious problems will be to break down any learning you want the children to acquire into steps small enough for them to take. It will be important to reward any progress, however small, with praise and encouragement. With children who have less serious difficulties, the task will be to make progress slowly, giving the children time to absorb each piece of new learning. It is also important not to create any negative emotional situations, even though the children make the same mistakes repeatedly. Always be positive and look for ways of fostering the children's self-esteem so that they believe they can learn and make progress.

Autism or Asperger's syndrome

There is some argument about whether these are two different conditions or much the same thing. Children who demonstrate these conditions are likely to show the following signs:

- difficulty in maintaining eye contact and lack of understanding of body language;
- difficulty in forming relationships and making friends;
- lack of understanding of other people's emotions and response to them;
- delay in language development;
- problems in understanding speech and a tendency to take things literally;
- lack of use of make-believe and imaginative play;
- intense preoccupation with particular interests that become obsessional.

The degree of this disability can be very varied, with some children having a good command of language and average intelligence and others having profound learning difficulties. As was suggested in the case study earlier in this chapter, such children need a very structured programme and environment and encouragement to make friends and to learn how to relate to others.

Dyslexia

Dyslexic children have difficulty with reading and spelling. They often make good contributions to discussion and are of good intelligence, but they have difficulty in matching the printed word to the spoken sounds. They may also have poor auditory memory and find difficulty in carrying out a sequence of instructions. They often find sequencing and organising ideas difficult. They also tend to make mistakes in pronunciation by expecting all words to be regular in their spelling.

Multi-sensory techniques are often useful with these children, perhaps hearing the word and repeating it, using tactile means of recognition by writing the word and remembering the movement of the hand. It may also help to think about the movements of the lips and tongue in saying the word. Another way of remembering particular spellings is to make up a short sentence in which each word starts with a particular letter that together spell a word the child is trying to learn. For example 'Sister Christine Has Only One Leg' is a way of remembering how to spell the word 'school'. Children often enjoy making up such sentences.

Another approach is to help a child remember words or syllables within words. For example, the word 'important' is made up of 'im' 'port' and 'ant' and you can remember it by picturing an 'ant' drinking 'port' from a bottle.

It is important to record children's difficulties in spelling as well as the words they can spell and read correctly so that you can try to think of ways of helping them to remember.

Dyspraxia

Some children appear to be clumsy and this is sometimes linked to dyslexia. This difficulty needs to be recognised and children may perhaps be given exercises to help them with their problems. They tend to have poor organisational skills, forgetting things and being generally disorganised. They often have no dominant hand and may write sometimes with the left hand and sometimes with the right. They may find it hard to keep still and they often disturb other children by moving clumsily and tripping over things. Such children are likely to have low self-esteem because their peers will tend to find them a nuisance. It is important to praise them whenever possible and encourage other children to be tolerant of them.

Attention deficit hyperactivity disorder (ADHD)

Some children with ADHD are inattentive, some are hyperactive and impulsive and some show all these characteristics. They are likely to have problems with paying attention and staying on task. They often lose things and are easily distracted. Some just cannot keep still and fidget all the time, often getting up and wandering about. They are impulsive and act without considering possible consequences and are often in trouble. They may also have problems in relating to other children and this can lead to a loss of self-esteem.

ADHD is often treated with Ritalin, which, though controversial, appears to work with many children. ADHD children need a highly structured environment in which there are clear routines that are followed daily. They should preferably be seated near the teacher and should be set clearly stated tasks. They should be observed and praised when they succeed in being on task for any reasonable length of time.

Sensory impairment

A child may have a hearing problem or a visual problem and both may, in the first place, be remedied by glasses or hearing aids. It is important that the child gets into the habit of using these aids, for some children will not want to reveal their difficulties to peers. You need to check each day that the aids are in use and working properly.

Visual problems may have affected the child's development if they are at all serious. The ability to move around freely and interact with different environments will affect the variety and range of the child's experience. Vision helps you to make sense of other sensory experiences and poor vision may affect this. It may make children less able to read body language and use it to communicate with others. It may also affect movement around the classroom and the school and create problems in physical education lessons. Reading will be problematic, and the child may need extra large type in reading material. A child may have colour blindness, and this can cause problems where colour is used to indicate the particular use of some things in the classroom. If you have children with very serious vision problems, you may find that their faces lack expression because they have not learned to read the expressions of others and imitate them.

Fortunately not many children have such serious problems, but you may have children who need extra help because they do not see well. They may need to be seated near the front so that they can see clearly writing on the board and projected material. You may also need to label things in larger type than you would usually use.

Hearing problems are less easy to discover, but you will get some indication about them from the child's reactions in class. If you think a child has a hearing problem then it is a good idea to test his or her hearing by speaking softly behind the child's back. If you find that the child cannot repeat what you said, then it is important that the parents' attention is drawn to the problem so that something can be done to help. Parents are likely to be aware of a problem and may need encouragement to seek remedies.

Children with physical disabilities

You may have some children in your class with various kinds of physical problems. If you are working with children who have previously been at a special school that has been closed and amalgamated with your school, staff from the special school may be able to advise you on how best to make provision that allows such children to make progress and become part of the class. There may be some children in wheelchairs, and you will need to organise your classroom with them in mind. You will also need to think about what part they can play in physical education lessons, and you may need advice from a physiotherapist on this. They need to move as much as they can in order to improve their mobility. You may also need to ensure that they have chairs and tables at heights that enable them to write easily. Try to be sensitive to the problems they may encounter in moving about the classroom and school.

It is important to treat all such children as normally as possible and encourage other children to do this, too. They should be included wherever possible in school visits and journeys. Thomas *et al.* (1998) note that research suggests that 'inclusive settings were less likely to induce a poor self-image than segregated ones. Moreover, counselling and efforts aimed at increasing sensitivity of both teachers and able-bodied students could help to abate feelings of difference that did exist' (p. 67).

Children who pose behaviour problems

This, in many ways, is one of the most difficult groups to help. They will tend to be disruptive and disturb other children, display temper upon occasions when things are not to their liking and find it difficult to settle to work. They are also likely to be unpopular with their peers, usually because they are not sensitive to the feelings of others. Some will be bullies and others are likely to be bullied and this may lead to conflict.

The best way of dealing with such children is to have clear rules for behaviour and to set them targets of getting through the morning or afternoon without a display of temper or swearing or transgressing the rules. Try using a chart on which you record behaviour by marking the chart each time the child succeeds in meeting the target and offering a reward of some kind if they can get through a week without misbehaving. It may be a good idea to involve parents in this by sending a letter when they achieve an agreed period without problems. Parents might then provide the reward.

You also need to talk to the child about anger management. Explain that when you feel angry you should perhaps count to ten and then try to think of something pleasant. It may help if, when the child shows a display of temper, you can ask a teaching assistant to take him or her to a quiet place, listen to what the child has to say about the situation and help him or her to think of something different. It may also be useful to discuss how the child thinks s/he has made other people feel.

Questions to think about

1 How much do I know about the particular problems of the children in my class who have special educational needs? How can I find out more?

2 How far am I succeeding in including children with various kinds of disability in the work of the class?

3 What am I doing to foster friendship between children with disabilities and other children?

4 To what extent am I managing my class in a way that integrates those with special educational needs? Can I do any more to achieve this?

5 What am I doing to make children with special educational needs feel part of the class? What can I do to help other children to relate well to them?

6 Children with special educational needs tend to have low self-esteem. Can I do more to combat this?

7 Am I doing enough to combat bullying?

8 Am I working well with LSAs and teaching assistants? Am I giving them enough help?

9 What records am I, and any assistants I have, keeping of children with special educational needs? Am I recording the most useful things for being able to help them?

10 Do the children with special educational needs in my class have all the equipment they need to help them work as normally as possible?

Chapter 7

Working with very able children

Identifying very able children

Many classes will contain some children who are much more able than the majority. It is important that such children are identified and that provision is made for them to extend their learning beyond the average stages. Research suggests that this does not always happen and such children often underperform in order not to appear different from their peer group.

If you teach the youngest children, you may be able to learn from parents when a very able child enters your class. Perhaps s/he is already reading simple texts, can write his or her name, has shown great interest in books or in some particular activity such as music or drawing and already seems to be in advance of his or her age group in interests and performance. It is also worth talking with the parents of a child of any age who shows unusual ability. What does the child do at home? How old was s/he when s/he started to talk? Did s/he show an early interest in reading, perhaps starting to read long before s/he started school? Has the child shown evidence of any unusual gifts or interests? Do the parents appear to support the child's interests and hobbies and give him or her a chance to develop them further? How does s/he get on with other children? What does the home background appear to be? What qualities do the parents seem to show? What about other children in the family – are there others who seem to be very able? It is important to work with the parents to develop the child's abilities. Try to make them partners in the child's education.

The next part of assessing such children involves careful observation. Potential intellectual giftedness is likely to become evident in the use of a large vocabulary, a high level of curiosity and the ability to learn rapidly and to concentrate intensively. Out of school interests may give you a clue to ability, and observation of their performance in class will give you clues about unusual levels of ability. Do they write more than other children? Do they have an unusually wide vocabulary? Do they appear to have more ideas? Do they concentrate well? Do they show intellectual curiosity and appear to have better powers of reasoning than their peer group? Is there evidence of an unusual imagination? Or creativity? Or skill in problem-solving? They should be given work that taxes their abilities, with quite a lot of scope for choosing how to develop it. It is important to recognise that gifted children have individual traits and need to be treated differently from each other, taking their particular strengths into account. They may also have strengths in several areas. They need opportunities to reveal their abilities and then encouragement to develop them.

An important characteristic of gifted children is creativity. They may suggest unusual ideas and solutions and original approaches. They tend to be more questioning and challenging than other children.

There may also be test results that give the child's IQ. You need to test both verbal and non-verbal abilities to get a useful result. If the results of two such tests are widely different, you may be dealing with a child who is underachieving. You then need to look carefully at how the child is doing. Is s/he showing strengths in areas that use verbal skills but not non-verbal skills or vice versa? Does s/he show strengths in mathematics? What can you do to raise attainment in the weaker areas?

Are the tests you used likely to be more difficult for a child from an ethnic minority background, or one who has learned to speak and read English only very recently? Is there evidence from the items the child got wrong that this was the case?

The needs of any child who scores 130 or over in an IQ test should be carefully considered. A score of 140+ shows an ability of about one in a thousand, and higher scores than this will show an even rarer level of ability. Research has found that very able children are often fitter, taller and heavier than average. They are also quite often the oldest child in the family.

Where younger children are concerned, you need to rely more on your own assessment. A very able child may have a high level of reading and comprehension at an early stage. Some able and rapid silent readers may not be good at reading aloud and can be misjudged. You can make judgements in such cases by questioning such children about the books they have read to judge comprehension.

You do not only need to be alert to children with high intellectual ability. Children may have high ability or talent in other areas. They may have physical talents and show exceptional promise in physical education and games. They may be more developed physically than the peer group and able to move particularly well. Such children may show early ability in basic physical skills such as running and jumping or throwing and catching. This may not be as evident in the early years as a high intellectual ability is, but you should encourage such children to practise physical skills, and if possible and if they are more physically developed than the peer group, perhaps provide some opportunities for them to join in with games involving older children.

Another child may have particular skills in music, art or technology. This will be evident from an early age in that the child will not only show interest in these areas but will perform at a level beyond that of his or her contemporaries. A musical child will sing in tune at a stage when others find this difficult, an artistic child will draw at a more advanced stage, and an inventive child will have exceptional ideas in technology. These skills need to be encouraged.

Some children are socially gifted. They appear to be more sensitive to others than most young children and to have more advanced ideas about other people. They work and play well with their contemporaries and often show leadership skills, tending to lead others when working in a group or in play.

There is some evidence that teachers do not always recognise exceptional ability or talent and that even when it is recognised, there is a lack of special provision to enable such children to perform to their full potential. This may be because the special needs of the gifted tend to be given less attention than the special needs of those with learning or other difficulties. Able children have very real needs, and unless these are identified early, a child may fail to reach his or her potential. While the really exceptional child is fairly rare, there are likely to be children in your class who are a good deal more able than the majority. You need to be aware of such children and try to give them some individual attention. They will ask demanding questions, have original ideas, be quick to absorb new concepts and be able to ask searching questions; they will be inventive and often demanding. They need encouragement and interest in their ideas and opportunities to explore and learn independently. Primary classrooms are busy places, and it is all too easy to be concerned about getting through the planned programme of class work, which the most able usually do well, and to give extra attention to the slow learners but fail to do very much for the very able. They are often expected to do the same rather repetitive work as other children, and they become bored with work that is much too easy and does not make any demand on them. They need to be extended and have opportunities to work at a higher and more demanding level than the majority. Gifts and talents become evident only if children have opportunities to demonstrate them. Success and satisfaction should be your constant aim. Lack of such opportunities may lead to boredom and time-wasting.

Personal and social development

Exceptionally able children – those with IQs of 145+ – may find it difficult to get on with their peers because they have little in common: the higher the IQ the greater the problem. Able children need the stimulus of children of similar abilities from time to time, and in a school where there are a number of such children, it may be a good idea to take groups of them out of class for more advanced work from time to time, if it can be managed. While it is important that they learn to get on with everybody, they also need opportunities to work with other very able children. Such children sometimes need the reassurance that an equally able group can give that they are normal and that there are others who share their interests. We should be aiming at giving these children the opportunity to fulfil their full potential, and this means enabling them to develop self-confidence.

As was suggested in an earlier chapter, there is a case for giving very able children some opportunities for working with older children with whom they may have more in common than children of their own age group.

Wallace (1983) quotes a nine-year-old on the feeling that he is alone: 'I am the loneliest person in the world because I really should be in the twenty-first century. I'm inventing things now but I have to wait until I'm grown-up because no one will listen to me' (p. 10). She goes on to describe his longing for a friend, for someone he can share his ideas with, but other children find his conversation confusing and overpowering and he has developed the habit of talking *at* any adult who is patient enough to listen. The needs of the exceptionally gifted are different from those of the moderately gifted, who are more likely to find ways of making friends and getting on with their age-group peers.

On the other hand, some very able children may have considerable powers of leadership and may create situations, when working in a group, in which they are the people with the ideas and they are able to persuade others to go along with them. However, in some cases, other children may find the ideas of the very able too complicated and not want to be involved with them. This is something of a test of the able child's leadership abilities.

Problems of getting on with the peer group may have an effect on the self-esteem of these children. An important aspect of self-concept is the perception of what others think of you. Very gifted children may have to come to terms with not being very popular. It is easy to assume that a very able person should have high self-esteem, but in practice they will also have high standards, which make them self-critical. You need to give thought to this and also to the opposite danger, which is that they may become too self-confident and opinionated, which is more likely in the case of a child who is able, but not exceptionally so.

Making provision for children of exceptional ability

It is important in dealing with these children to help them to become independent learners as soon as possible. Learning how to learn is important for all children, but for the very able it is essential. There is a limit to how much teacher attention you can give them, and they need to be able to learn on their own, perhaps while the rest of the class do easier work. The skills involved include the ability to take meaning from reading or listening and, at a later stage, making notes from text. They also need skills in working with ICT. They then need to be able to sort out their ideas and put them in order and use this list as a guide to writing or making a presentation. They also need the skills of problem-solving, not only to solve mathematical problems but also to solve those in technology and more generally. These skills need to be taught to all children at an appropriate stage, but the very able will need them much earlier than their peers.

You can provide opportunities for such children in whole-class work by asking questions that can be answered at different levels. Wallace (1983) quotes the following questions asked by a teacher in a mathematics lesson, which give quite a wide range of opportunities:

> What do you think happens if …?
> Can you find the pattern?
> Is the pattern always the same?
> Can you discover the rule?
> Can you reverse the rule?

(p. 6)

These are questions that provoke thinking for a wide range of children.

Boys and girls tend to show their ability rather differently. There is some evidence that suggests that teachers tend to notice, reward and encourage boys to a much greater extent than they do girls, even when the boys show somewhat deviant behaviour. Girls tend to hold back in discussion and a number in the very able category are not much noticed because they are quiet and not attention-seeking. Girls also tend to feel social pressure not to ask too many questions or pursue their ideas too actively. Girls tend to be more conformist than boys. This means that teachers need to be on the lookout for girls who are very able but so quiet that their ability is not always noticed.

As a teacher you need to remember that in dealing with able children – especially any who you feel are more able than you are – you need to be aware that you could feel threatened by a really exceptional child. You may feel it difficult to advise such a child because s/he always seems to get there before you. Research has found that in some cases, teachers are not prepared to admit that a child is exceptional and feel it may not be good for the child to be treated differently from others because of his or her ability. There is also evidence that some teachers tend to be antagonistic to gifted children, thinking it is not good for them to be praised too much or encouraged to do work at a more advanced level than their peers. This could be a waste of the children's potential. Such children may do great things when they grow up; they can be very rewarding if you take time to listen to their ideas and provide opportunities for them to pursue them.

A particular type of very able child is rather easy to miss. This type of child is quiet and unassuming and does neat pages of sums that are all correct. If this is happening fairly frequently, you need to ask yourself whether the work is too easy. Does the child need more challenging work? Could s/he tackle more difficult problems? Does s/he need more individual work? Very often the written work of such children shows unusual features, a more advanced vocabulary and more original ideas. Can you help him or her to develop such ideas further?

Not all gifted children are earnest students, working well and being keen to learn. Some are aggressive and disruptive, calling out in class, producing very untidy work that is often hard to read. They may find it helpful to be able to present some of their written work on a computer. It is often difficult to be sympathetic to such children, and yet they are expressing their needs in their behaviour and showing that they are dissatisfied with what is happening to them.

You need to be aware of your own reactions, especially when you are getting to know a new class. Their previous teacher may have told you that a particular child is very able, and you may get the impression that the child has become a bit conceited because the teacher has shown extra interest in his or her work. Working with such children is not easy. The important thing is to remain sensitive and aware and to be prepared to provide for such a child a path that will extend his or her learning.

If appropriate provision is to be made for gifted children you will need to study how they learn. You also need to seek out ways of developing creativity.

There are a number of difficult choices to make about these children, some at school level and most at class level. At school level you need to decide if acceleration is ever

Dealing with a difficult yet able child

Martin had been a trial to every teacher he had encountered. He was restless and often wandered about the classroom, disturbing other children. He almost never put up his hand to answer or ask a question, preferring to call out. He always wanted to do something in a different way from everyone else and he was unpopular with the other children. His work was scrappy and difficult to read although, when you could make out what he was trying to say, it was interesting. In maths his work, when you could decipher it, was usually correct, and he often worked at high speed, usually finishing before everyone else. His parents found him difficult too because he was a problem at home and his room was always a mess.

When he got to Year 4 the teacher, Brenda, went to the head and suggested that Martin should see a psychologist to see if anything could be done to help him. This was arranged with his parents' agreement, and appointments were made. He came back enthusiastic about his sessions with the psychologist and said 'He seemed to understand me.'

A few days later the report came. It said that Martin had an IQ of 150 and was almost certainly underachieving in school. Martin had said he did not like school much. The work was always too easy and boring. No one seemed to be interested in the things that interested him, one of which the psychologist found to be archaeology – he discovered that Martin had a profound knowledge of this subject, something that had never come out in school. The psychologist concluded that Martin's behaviour problems were the result of the lack of challenge and interest in the work he was expected to do. He suggested that Martin should be given more demanding work and encouraged to pursue his interest in archaeology. He also promised to visit the school and talk with Martin's teacher about his needs.

Brenda found this report interesting and revealing. After talking with the psychologist she talked at length with Martin and started to plan a programme for him that involved him in seeking out information for himself more frequently and gave him the opportunity to work on his particular interests. She borrowed books on archaeology from the public library for him to read and encouraged him to make notes from them and use the information to compile his own book on the subject. He really enjoyed doing this and gradually became much less of a problem in class.

to be a possible solution for the child who is way above the standards of his age group. This will be a fairly rare occurrence, because children of this ability are rare, but there may be a case for it. It is not common in British schools to promote very able children beyond their age group. There are many disadvantages to this, but evidence from other countries where this is practised suggests that a very able child gets on better with older children with whom the child has more interests in common than s/he does with contemporaries. It is a possibility to be considered in a very few rare cases.

Gross (2004) describes work with a group of really exceptional children in an Australian school who were placed in a class of older children. The researchers found that the exceptional children had more in common with those in their new class and made better progress than children of similar ability who were not accelerated. They also found that the children in question said that the loneliness and boredom they had found in their age-group class disappeared when they were with an older group. So acceleration should not be completely dismissed. However, it may be easier to offer additional provision for a very able group culled from several classes who can be withdrawn for extra teaching on a regular basis. Although this may not be easy to staff, it may be a solution. This is often done for children with learning difficulties, and very able children also have special educational needs.

Another question to be decided is whether there should be ability grouping. Very able children have a lot to offer to a group, and this may be lost if they are always in a separate working group. At the same time they need the stimulus of being with other able children. There is a case for using ability grouping and groups of mixed ability at different times.

Another possibility is the enrichment of the general programme. It may be useful to ask children, particularly any who you suspect are very able, to complete a questionnaire that asks the child to make a self-assessment. Like the one suggested in Chapter 4, this questionnaire could ask children what they think they are good at and what they would like to know more about. It could also ask about particular interests out of school and anything they would particularly like to study. You can then plan suitable topics with very able children, using the information from the questionnaire as a guide. They can pursue the topic independently after discussing with you how they will work.

The topics chosen may be related to those that the class is studying but extended and taken to a different level, or they may be related or unrelated topics chosen by the child in consultation with you. This will involve exploring the child's particular interests and taking into consideration the resources you have available. You may be able to find or encourage a child to find material on the internet. Where you have more than one very able child a group may be able to share a topic and plan work on it together. They might be asked to plan a presentation to the class of their findings.

Another element in provision is the fostering of creativity, getting children to think of and develop ideas. Questions such as these might lead to some inventive ideas:

- What is likely to happen in fifty years' time and why do you think this?
- Imagine you were lost in a forest and had no idea where you were. What would you do?
- How do you think an animal as strange as a tortoise evolved?

The ease with which children come up with solutions would depend on their age and stage of development as well as their creative ability and general intelligence.

Such questions could be set for discussion in pairs and the solutions discussed with the whole class. You also need to be alert to unusual interests and take the opportunity to encourage children who show evidence of such interests to produce work based on them, perhaps looking for books that would extend the interest and provide the background for further exploration. Such work might be made into a booklet and become part of the class library.

Most gifted children, but especially boys, are interested in using computers and are often very knowledgeable about them. A booklet such as that suggested above can be compiled on a computer; this can give scope for illustrations as well as writing, and the use of typed script instead of handwriting makes the booklet more easily readable for other children.

Questions to think about

1 Have I any children in my class who are gifted or talented? What is the evidence for this? What are their particular gifts and talents?
2 What provision should I make for them? What are their strengths?
3 What are their particular interests? Can I use these for their further learning?
4 How do they get on with other children? Do they tend to be loners? Do I need to do something to help their social development?

continued

5 Do they have opportunities to work with other able children as well as opportunities to work in mixed groups?

6 Have I been able to learn more about them from their parents? Do I work with the parents to help them to make good provision for their children?

7 Are there any children in my class who may be gifted and underachieving? Is there a chance that I am missing some of them, perhaps because they do not want to reveal themselves as different?

8 What level of self-esteem have the children who seem to be very able? Am I showing them that I value their work and abilities?

9 Am I able to provide a programme of enrichment and creativity for very able children?

10 What am I doing to enable the children in my class, particularly the very able, to learn independently? How successful am I being?

11 Are there more boys than girls in this category? Am I missing some very able girls because they are less in evidence than boys?

12 What records am I keeping of the progress of gifted children? What can I learn from them?

Chapter 8

Children from other cultures

People from other countries and other cultures have been arriving in Britain for many years. Some children entering school now will be from families who have been here for more than one generation. Others will be more recent arrivals. Asylum seekers are currently entering the country in some numbers. Many schools will now have substantial numbers of children of other cultures in every class. While those coming from families who have been settled here for some years will probably speak fluent English, others may have only a smattering of the language and this poses problems for teachers.

Knowledge of other cultures

Teachers working in an area where there are many immigrant children need to find out as much as they can about the cultures from which the children come. They should have some knowledge of the customs that are current in each culture, its history and traditions, its religion, its language, the accepted dress and the food the children are used to. Teachers need to know what is considered to be polite behaviour in each culture so that they do not offend parents by failing to observe this or get the impression that children are being difficult when they behave in ways that are acceptable in their own culture but not in school. For example, in some cultures children are not expected to make eye contact with adults other than family and this can be disconcerting to a teacher. You also need to be aware that the children may have different ways of behaving from indigenous British children that may seem to some teachers to be out of line. This is particularly true of Afro-Caribbean boys, who are often thought to be cheeky when behaving in a way that would be acceptable at home.

Multicultural education and racism

Racism is a problem that you need to combat wherever you find it. You may have some racial prejudices yourself, including some of which you are not aware, and you may also find prejudice in some of your colleagues. Face these views if you hold them and consider your evidence for them carefully. Are you generalising from a small sample? How did you come to hold such views? Do any of the children you teach have racial prejudices? If so, what can you do about it?

Today's children live in a country where there is a good deal of racism that needs to be combated and a population that is racially mixed. All schools, whatever their population, need to provide multicultural education. The best way of doing this is to discuss the reasons why we should be welcoming to people of other races, avoiding stereotypes and accepting that different people have different customs and ways of living and these are just as acceptable as anything we do ourselves. Try to see that books that represent this view are available to the children. This will not be altogether easy because some children may have parents who hold racist views and pass them on to their children. Such parents may also object to multicultural teaching and tackle you about it.

Case study

Joanna and Marilyn taught two parallel Year 5 classes and decided that they would like to work together and share a topic, with each class taking a different viewpoint with the needs of a particular group of children in mind. In both classes there were many Pakistani children, and the teachers wanted to do some work that would boost their confidence and help to make them feel that their culture was valued by the school. They also wanted to help the other children to know about the background of their Pakistani peer group. They decided that one class would study the geography of Pakistan and the other class Pakistani history, culture and customs. At the end of the work each class would prepare a presentation for the other class and create an exhibition that would go on show in the school entrance hall.

There was some individual work within such a topic to match the abilities and interests of the children and also a good deal of group work in which Pakistani children shared their knowledge with others. This was helpful to the Pakistani children for whom English was a second language in that they were happy to contribute within a group where they had the advantage of some inside knowledge, although they too had much to learn about their country of origin.

The children were encouraged to bring to school items of Pakistani costume and artefacts, which helped to illustrate their work. They also taught the other children some of their language and demonstrated some behavioural customs.

The shared presentations gave a purpose to the work, and the teachers agreed that each class should evaluate the work of the other and give a report on it. This would help the children to be self-critical about their work.

Check whether you treat children of any particular background differently. There is a good deal of evidence that teachers sometimes treat Afro-Caribbean boys differently, perhaps punishing them more harshly than white boys who have done something similar, and often giving them fewer chances to answer questions in class. Are you ever guilty of being patronising to a child from another culture, perhaps saying something like 'That's very good for you', implying that you did not expect much? Do you ever attribute undesirable traits to all children from a particular racial group such as Afro-Caribbeans, assuming that because some of them misbehave and underachieve, they all will? Labelling and stereotyping are sure recipes for making these things happen.

If you work in a multicultural school multicultural education is more likely to make sense to parents and there is the opportunity to get children of different cultures or their parents to tell the class about their way of life. Do all you can to find things to applaud about other cultures and look for good things about their customs.

Multicultural resources

Books, pictures and other materials should reinforce the multicultural message. A textbook, reference book or story book should support the identity, experience and concerns of ethnic minority children and challenge ideas about whites being superior in any way.

You also need to look critically at story books and other books in the class and school library to see if the text or pictures imply this. The need for critical thinking about relationships in books and materials also applies to male and female representation. Are men or boys represented as in any way superior to women? Is it suggested that women have more limited life choices than men?

The achievement of different cultural groups

There are seven main groups of cultures in our schools – Indian, Pakistani, Bangladeshi, Chinese, black African, black Afro-Caribbean and white. There are also asylum seekers who may be of European origin or come from other areas. The advent of asylum seekers in considerable numbers is too recent to allow a clear picture of how they perform at school. Of the others, Chinese and Indian children usually do well and tend to rival and sometimes outperform white children, who normally do better than other groups. The other groups do less well and often underachieve. In the first place, this may be because English is a second language for many of them. It may also be that the use of English at school is different from the use of English in a child's home and s/he needs time to come to terms with this. There may be underachievement by some groups who have acquired fluent English and there may be some groups who had to learn English as a second language who achieve really well.

The groups who most often underachieve are Afro-Caribbean and black African children. Pakistani and Bangladeshi children also tend to do less well and this shows up in the Standard Attainment Tasks (SATs) tests at Key Stage 1 and also at Key Stage 2. These children often go on to underperform at GCSE level. However, although this is frequently the case, it is important not to work expecting this pattern with a new class. Studies of the achievement of different groups suggest that in some areas African, Afro-Caribbean, Pakistani and Bangladeshi children do well.

Teacher and parent expectation

Teacher and parent expectation is an important factor and you need to think how you can communicate the idea that you expect good work, even from children who normally lag behind. 'Good work' in this sense may describe the best that an individual child can do, even if the child's performance is lower than that of many of the class. The idea is to emphasise that you expect progress and offer praise and encouragement when it is achieved. Never imply that you do not expect much from a particular group or a particular child.

Black Afro-Caribbean children

The parents of Afro-Caribbean children have high expectations of their children and support them well, but this still leaves them as the lowest performing group and in many ways the most difficult group for behaviour, and there can be a high level of conflict with teachers. A consequence of this is that teachers come to expect poor behaviour from the boys in particular, and there is a tendency to blame them for anything that goes wrong. Consequently they are sometimes unfairly treated, which causes resentment. A substantial number (28 per cent) in the London area have been found to have special educational needs, and this has often turned out to be not justified. There is some evidence that parents feel that the reasons why their children perform badly is the result of racism on the part of teachers. Teachers have low expectations and the children perform accordingly.

A study of the experiences of black boys carried out in London (London Development Agency 2004) found that the boys received a high level of negative attention and a low level of positive attention from teachers. The study concluded that the experience of school for these boys was poor. They found the curriculum barren and boring, especially in the secondary school, and the relationship with teachers was characterised by conflict. This was true for all age groups. Teachers did not listen to them, and they felt that their experiences were different from those of white children. Black girls were slightly more positive and felt that they were treated differently from the boys. Both boys and girls found that black teachers were more encouraging and supportive and expected more from them. The boys' ideas for improving the situation were as follows:

- Teachers should take more interest in them and listen to them.
- There was a need for teacher training to deal with black children.
- There should be more black teachers.
- Black Afro-Caribbean boys should be trusted more.
- There should be small after-school classes for them.
- Courses should be more creative.

(p. 51)

Other strategies suggested by the study to raise black children's attainment were as follows:

- a strong emphasis on high quality teaching;
- many opportunities for students to explore their cultural heritage;
- good data analysis;
- working closely with parents.

(p. 113)

In most groups girls tend to outperform boys, as we saw in an earlier chapter, although this may not always be the case. Social class also has a considerable effect on performance. Middle-class children do better than those from working-class families, although this is less marked in the case of Afro-Caribbean children.

The Ethnic Minority Achievement Grant (EMAG)

The work of teachers dealing with children from ethnic minorities, especially those with English as a second language has been helped considerably by the EMAG, which was set up in 1999 to provide assistance and advice for teachers on the backgrounds of children and on some of the difficulties facing them. LEAs were obliged to devolve 85 per cent of the funding for ethnic minorities to schools and to provide training for both specialist and mainstream staff. The key elements of the work of EMAG staff involve a focus on attainment of ethnic minority pupils and concern for their underachievement.

This has been particularly helpful in the case of asylum-seeker children, who may come to school with very little understanding of the British way of life and with no knowledge of English. There have been particular problems when teachers have had no access to interpreters or to EMAG staff. Where there has been this kind of assistance, teachers have been given information about each child's competence in his or her home language. They have also had access to advice on the placing of these children in year groups and classes as well as information about their previous educational experience. Teachers have also been able to give advice to parents on entitlements such as free school meals, and some have helped parents to get computer access to newspapers in their home language. EMAG staff have also supported schools during admissions and sometimes helped in classrooms. They have worked with teachers to provide classroom support, liaised with families and helped to train other staff to work with these children.

Ethnic minority teachers

While schools have acknowledged the value of having some black and other ethnic minority teachers, the teachers themselves have found problems. They have found racism among colleagues and parents, difficulties in getting promotion, lack of support for professional development and being expected to solve all the problems other teachers found with black and ethnic minority pupils. They have had a feeling of isolation in the school. Some white parents have felt that black teachers were incapable of teaching their children. There has been a need for induction for black teachers from overseas and a need to simplify the route to Qualified Teacher Status.

The ethnic minority children themselves have been enthusiastic about black teachers. They have felt that they understood them in a way that other teachers did not and thought it was important that schools recruited more black teachers.

Assessment and evaluation

Schools need to assess the performance of their children by ethnic group as well as by gender and ability, to keep track of how well different groups are doing and to identify which groups are doing less well. This helps to determine where more effort perhaps needs to be made to ensure that all children are reaching their potential.

It is very easy for teachers and others to see an individual child as representative of a group (especially where there are few children of the child's race in the class) and to take the child's attitudes and behaviour as typical of the children of that background. It is important to see each child as an individual, each with his or her own attitudes, ways of behaving, abilities and potential and to help him or her develop to the fullest extent possible.

Individual records need to record observations made in the course of daily work as well as assessments made over a longer period. This is not easy to do in a busy class-room but is worth doing. If you keep a note pad handy and make a one-word note of something significant you have observed, along with the child's initials, perhaps, this should enable you to record it in more detail later. Look out for unusual answers or comments, a child who has made an important step in understanding, or one using the correct English word or phrase for the first time. All these observations help you to find ways of extending learning for individuals as well as for the class. Classroom assistants can help with this process too if you explain what you are trying to do.

Children learning English as an additional language

Many teachers have to face this problem, which may be particularly difficult where a school is taking in a considerable number of asylum seekers' children, who may be starting with no knowledge of the English language or British customs. It is a considerable help if some EMAG or bilingual teachers can work with classroom teachers to support and advise them. Much thought needs to be given to ways of making the newcomers feel part of the class and school. It may be tempting to pass the problem over to EMAG or bilingual teachers, but class teachers need to give a lot of thought to ways of including all children as much as possible. It is also important to show that the child's home language is valued: perhaps you could ask them to share with the class their words for greetings or for colours or numbers at the same time as you give them the English equivalent words; and you could let the English-speaking children have a go at using the home language words of the English as an Additional Language (EAL) learners. If you have the help of an EMAG or bilingual teacher it is useful to find out each child's skill in his or her first language and how that language differs from English. For example, it is useful to know whether the child's first language is written from left to right or right to left, since you may need to explain such differences when the children start to write. You also need to know something about the social language and behaviour of your ethnic minority children such as greetings, thanks and introductions so that you can explain the British customs.

There is much to be said for children having a chance to discuss things in their own language in pairs or groups in the process of learning new English words and phrases. This is an opportunity for them to help each other to understand what is required of them. There may also be a case for pairing an English speaking child with one learning English on other occasions. It can be a useful experience for the English speaker to try to explain new words to a partner. It is a chance to practise defining things so that someone else can understand. It may be a good idea to talk about this with the class and suggest ways in which they can help the newcomers.

In the literacy hour you can sometimes work with the whole class and sometimes group children so that you can work with those learning English as an additional language while the teaching assistant works with the English-speaking children. When you work with the whole class you can collect words of a particular kind, such as colour words, number words, words describing characteristic and feelings, such as happy, clever, funny, lonely and so on, perhaps using illustrations of some of them with word or sentence labels. This can be useful to the English-speaking children in exploring the words they might use in a later piece of writing with an accent on using adjectives well, perhaps to describe a person or a situation. For the non-English speakers it can add words to their spoken and written vocabulary. It will also be important to teach short phrases and sentences using the new words they are learning.

Non-verbal behaviour is important in dealing with children learning a new language. Actions such as pointing, showing a picture, smiling or acting out something can be helpful. The English-speaking members of the class can often make useful suggestions about how to demonstrate the meaning of words by actions and can perhaps act out particular words from time to time for the EAL children to see if they can understand. Pictures with word or sentence labels are useful, and a big book with pictures and very limited vocabulary may be used to introduce a simple story, which the children can discuss in their own language(s) and can try to retell in response to questions about the people in the story and what happened to them.

A particularly difficult situation is when there are only one or two children in the class who need to learn English. This is a situation where the help of an EMAG or bilingual teacher is particularly welcome as s/he will be able to work with the individual(s) while you work with the rest of the class. However, you need to be constantly on the look out for ways in which such children can be made to feel part of the class and learn from others. It will be important to be welcoming to the EAL child and to encourage the English-speaking children to be welcoming, perhaps pairing the new child or children with English-speaking partners who can try to teach the newcomers some English words and make sure that they are not left out at playtime.

Questions to think about

1   How much do I know about the home culture of the children in my class? What sources of information have I about this? How can I best use this knowledge?

2   Have I any stereotypic views of children of any particular background? Have I any racist views that I am not fully aware of? Do these affect the way I treat particular children?

3   Am I doing enough to integrate children of different racial background into the class? Am I encouraging white children to hold a non-racist view and to accept others as individual people who are valuable in their own right?

4   Do I treat any group of children or any individuals in a different way from the rest of the class without justification?

5   How do the books available in my classroom represent people of other cultures?

6   Do I compare the performance of children of different cultural groups so that I can be aware of any groups that are not doing well?

7   Do black children, especially boys, pose any particular problems? How should I deal with these?

8   Have I children in my class for whom English is an additional language? How can I best provide for them?

9   If I have the help of an EMAG teacher or a bilingual teacher, how can I make best use of his or her assistance?

10   How do we, as a staff, treat teachers from ethnic minorities?

Chapter 9

Children from different social backgrounds

Children's social background has a considerable effect on their schooling. Middle-class children come to school accepting, to a large extent, the routines and demands the school makes because their parents have prepared them for the idea that school is important for their futures. In many cases they have been accustomed to a fairly organised life at home. Working-class children, on the other hand, are more likely to find it difficult to accept school routine. They tend to set a low value on their education although many working-class parents want their children to have a good education. This does not mean that middle-class children are necessarily always easier to teach than working-class children, but the problems they pose tend to be rather different.

Children's social background has an important effect on their lives and their ability to gain from their education. Generally speaking, social background has a stronger effect than gender or culture. The life chances for children from working-class families are poorer than those for children from middle-class families, although there will always be those who do well and succeed by sheer ability and persistence.

The take-up of free school meals is the only independent indication of social background available, but even this may not always be a good indicator of social class. There will be middle-class children who do not come from affluent homes and may be the children of single parents. Teachers will be only too aware of the kinds of background from which their children come. Children's speech will give an indication of social background. Working-class children also come to school with fewer of the skills that contribute to their learning than middle-class children. Middle-class children will probably have been read to and encouraged to take an interest in books and will perhaps be able to read some words and read and write their own names before they start school. There will have been books and probably computers in the home. They are more likely to have had a fairly ordered home life and had less freedom than working-class children, who may be accustomed to playing in the streets and thus be more streetwise and who may grow up in certain ways more quickly.

The make-up of the school catchment area

The balance of children from different social backgrounds will vary with the catchment area, and this will have an important effect on the school. Connolly (2004) describes two schools in Northern Ireland, one in a middle-class area and one in a working-class area. The school in the working-class area placed strong emphasis on pastoral issues, feeling that the children needed help in developing appropriate behaviour for school. Some of the parents were unhappy with this because they felt that their children were not getting a 'proper' education, which they tended to define as sitting still and doing what the teacher told them to do. The middle-class school, on the other hand, moved to a more formal approach fairly quickly, because the parents wanted it and the children could take it and profit by it. The school also emphasised academic success. The children, particularly the boys, tended to be competitive.

The two school staffs had different views of parents and the parents had different views of the schools. The working-class parents, many of whom were unemployed or single parents, were often stressed by the effects of poverty and lived something of a hand-to-mouth existence. They tended to lack the confidence to approach teachers and were defensive in talking to them. They often lacked knowledge of what was happening in the school and were not in a position to support their children's learning. The middle-class parents, on the other hand, had no such inhibitions. Their interest in education and their views of its value tended to be passed on to their children, who adapted more easily to school than their working-class peers. The middle-class children often put pressure on their children to succeed and pressure on the teachers to help them. Most were deeply interested in what was going on at school and came to all the parents' meetings.

Teachers also had their own views of parents. They were sometimes defensive in talking to them, especially in the working-class school, where parents were critical of the emphasis placed on pastoral care and social skills. They wanted their children to do well, and they believed that the path to success was the formal education that they had experienced themselves, while the teachers felt that the children would respond better to informal methods. The teachers at the middle-class school often felt under pressure from parents who were ambitious for their children, but the relationship was a more equal one.

The children in these two schools had very different career aspirations. The working-class boys had aspirations for manual jobs such as building, fixing cars or cleaning carpets, whereas the middle-class boys aimed at either professional jobs, such as doctors or scientists, or fantasy jobs, such as footballers or TV presenters. Connolly does not say anything about the girls' ambitions.

Boys in these two schools were also influenced by the different views of masculinity that were current in their home background. As we saw in Chapter 5, masculinity in working-class areas tends to be concerned with physical strength. Boys enjoy fighting and wrestling with each other, and playground games are often of a violent nature. They look to adult employment in jobs that require physical strength. In middle-class areas there are elements of this too, but boys tend to see their future in more academic terms. They see themselves in more professional posts and come to appreciate the need for education if they are to achieve this kind of future.

Many of these differences tend to apply also to children from ethnic minorities, although the differences in upbringing also have a strong effect. Social class differences in achievement can also be seen in many of these children. These differences are not so pronounced in the case of Afro-Caribbean children, because they tend to do less well whatever their background, in spite of the fact that their parents are very keen for them to do well and do much to encourage them. If they are middle-class, they are the lowest attaining of all the middle-class groups and tend to be barely level with working-class children in other ethnic groups. When they are working-class, they are the lowest attaining of all. They also tend to get a reputation for being troublesome, and this leads to a certain amount of stereotyping on the part of teachers.

An important determinant of achievement is teacher expectation. Teachers of children from working-class areas may often find it difficult to expect a great deal from their children, because their experience suggests that most of them will not achieve as well as their middle-class peers. This is where it is important to set ambitious targets both for you and for the children and to strive to achieve them. You need to challenge any limited views you or they may hold. There will be some children from a working-class background who will go on to achieve well and end up in professional jobs. Children in the in-between groups particularly need to be challenged by ambitious targets (see p. 60: A working-class child who did well).

A working-class child who did well

Bob Jenkins came from a council estate where many parents were out of work. Bob's father was out of work, but his mother had a job stacking shelves in a supermarket. This meant that things at home were often disorganised, as his mother was rushed off her feet with her job and catering for five children. Bob was the middle child and from the time he started in reception he showed that he was brighter than his brothers and sisters and had ideas of his own. He took to reading like a duck to water and could not find enough books to satisfy his thirst for reading. He read stories and non-fiction books, many at a level well above that of his classmates. When talking to his teacher about books one day, she suggested that he should join the public library where there were hundreds of books. He was enthusiastic about this idea, and after school the next day he went to the library and asked how to join. They gave him a form to fill in and take home for his parents to sign. His parents were really surprised at this. None of the other children had shown any interest in reading, and neither parent read anything more complicated than the sports news. Bill revelled in the choice of books available to him at the library and went there every few days to change his books.

As Bob moved up the school he showed evidence of being a very able child. He wrote very good stories and could also write factual material. He did well in mathematics and science partly because of his reading of non-fiction and his interest in how things worked. His ideas for investigation were excellent and went well beyond anything his teacher had thought of. He decided he wanted to be a writer or a scientist when he grew up, and the school felt that he was well on the way to achieving this kind of ambition. When the time came for transfer to secondary school, the head teacher made a special point of contacting the secondary school and telling them about Bob's progress, hoping that they would do all they could to help him.

Bob did well at secondary school and got A grades in eight of the nine GCSE subjects he took. He went on to do A levels in English literature, biology and physics, and gained a place at university to read sciences.

Organising to cater for all abilities

A school with a mixed catchment area has the difficult problem of working out how to provide for the children's range of abilities and backgrounds. There may be children from working-class homes, some from middle-class homes and others who are in between. Working-class children may have two reactions to being in a mixed class. The girls, in particular, may become discouraged because they feel they do not do as well as the middle-class children. Older children, especially girls, may be self-conscious about their speech and perhaps their dress, if the school is not one where all children wear uniform. They may also feel that they are not as good as the middle-class children at school work. Boys may be less self-conscious about this and feel more confident with working-class speech, which for them may have overtones of masculinity. As teacher you need to be supportive and encouraging to children from all backgrounds but particularly the working-class children, who may need to be helped to develop self-esteem. It will be helpful to have some socially mixed groups from time to time so that the children learn to mix with each other, talk with each other and learn from each other.

Questions to think about

1 What is the social background of the children in my class? What effect does it appear to have on their behaviour and learning?

2 How many children in my class have free school meals?

3 Am I making assumptions about some children's ability because of their speech? Are these assumptions justified?

4 How competitive are the children in my class? Is their competitiveness having an adverse effect on some children?

5 How well do I know the parents of the children in my class? What is my impression of the degree of support each child gets at home?

6 Have any children parents who are pressuring them to achieve? Is this having a good or bad effect on the child in any particular case? Should I try to do anything about it?

7 Have any children parents who are not supporting them? What should I try to do about this?

8 If I have a class of older children, what career ambitions do they have? Do these reflect their social background? Are they realistic? Should I try to raise their expectations?

9 Have I any children from a working-class background who have real ability? How can I best support them?

10 What sorts of targets for achievement should I set for my children? Are the targets I set sufficiently ambitious to challenge them?

11 How can I best support and raise the self-esteem of children who come from poor homes?

Chapter 10

Personal, social and health education

The National Curriculum for personal, social and health education (PSHE) starts with the following statement:

> Personal, social and health education (PSHE) is part of the national curriculum and may come into the teaching of other subjects and is part of the way children are dealt with in school. There is an element of personal and social education in the way teachers deal with discipline problems and relationships and conflicts among children. The national curriculum (1999) states that PSHE and citizenship help to give the pupils the knowledge, skills and understanding they need to lead confident, healthy, independent lives and to become informed, active, responsible citizens.
>
> (The National Curriculum; Department for
> Education and Employment 1999)

This makes it clear that PSHE is an essential part of life in schools as well as a particular area of learning. Lang (1988) makes the following statement about the subject:

- It involves taking account of *physical* and *psychological development processes* as well as *socialisation* within families, school and other social institutions, including culture and social class.
- It has a *moral* component and is concerned with the development of values, attitudes and feelings as well as knowledge/understanding and behaviour and skills.
- It involves the growth of understanding and feelings about the self as an entity, as well as in relation to others and to the social groups of which one is a part.
- It concerns the development of competence in communication, in one-to-one relationships and in groups.
- It must be understood in the context of the relation of human beings to the natural world – especially, in the case of primary children, to animals and plants.
- It has implications for, and should be involved in many curriculum areas; other curriculum areas can also contribute to its development, particularly in terms of the pedagogical approach used.
- It has implications for those who teach it – among other things they will need to seek a degree of self-awareness and in some cases a certain amount of personal change may be required before a teacher can undertake effective work in this area.

(p. 12)

He also suggests that PSHE should help children communicate well, expressing their real feelings and discussing sensitive issues openly, and also help to make them sensitive to others and appreciative of their efforts and better able to help others and be cooperative. They should be more responsible as individuals, too.

The paper *Excellence and Enjoyment: Learning and Teaching in the Primary Years* (Department for Education and Skills 2004) suggests that children should learn to name and deal with their feelings positively, identifying the positive things about themselves, overcoming fears and meeting challenges. These skills are all part of PSHE as well as being a concern across the curriculum and a concern in dealing with children more generally. Every teacher should be concerned with children's emotional development as well as their physical and intellectual development. As teacher you need to be concerned with all your children as developing human beings, helping them to build their self-esteem and developing their relationships with others. The classroom should be a positive place where children learn to respect themselves and others.

PSHE is also concerned with health education, and the school can choose whether or not to teach sex education. Children in the later years of primary education are asking questions that need to be answered, and a good sex education programme will provide many of the answers for them. Health education should cover diet and exercise and ways of maintaining good health.

Child development

Children in the primary years are developing rapidly, physically, intellectually and socially. They need to come to terms with the people they are becoming, recognising their abilities and difficulties, and striving to make the most of the abilities and to overcome the difficulties. They will learn from the reactions of those around them how they are seen by others. This can be rewarding or disturbing and you need to be aware of children who find it difficult to get on with others, who are rarely chosen by others for teams in games or other team activities, and whom other children tend to show that they do not like. Such children need to be supported and encouraged to be helpful to others and to find ways of interacting with them in a positive way. You need to make a point of praising them when they are helpful and sympathetic to other children as well as looking for ways of reinforcing their self-esteem. You also need to work with all the children to determine their stages of development, their skills and knowledge, their difficulties, both academic and social, and the extent of their self-esteem and self-image. The self-image is initially formed by the reactions of parents and siblings and is then further developed by the reactions of teachers and other children. You need to consider the development of each child's self-image from time to time, perhaps in the context of discussing his or her overall progress. You will then have an idea of how much encouragement an individual child may need to reinforce his self-esteem.

The Berkshire LEA paper on personal and social education (1997) suggests that schools should encourage pupils to:

- develop a sense of worth, self-esteem and self-awareness and confidence and to be self-critical;
- learn and apply appropriate behaviour in a range of situations and circumstances;
- develop confidence and sensitivity in cooperating, negotiating, seeing things from more than one point of view and resolving conflict;
- gain satisfaction and enjoyment from being contributing members of the school and the wider community;
- develop adaptability, flexibility and the ability to exercise initiative;
- develop an increasing awareness of and responsibility towards the immediate and wider community;
- take responsibility for their own learning.

(p. 5)

There is a strong case for using such a list to assess how far your children are developing these abilities and ensuring that you provide opportunities for practising such skills. You also need to consider the attitudes and values you want the children to develop and consider ways in which you can support this development. The Berkshire paper suggests that you need to consider ways of developing tolerance, respect, compassion, reliability and trustworthiness, and greater awareness of other people's feelings and respect for the views of others.

Group work and communication skills

Many of these attitudes require good communication skills, and this is an important aim at all levels. Schools are becoming increasingly aware of the need for children to talk together about what they are learning and to develop the ability to do this in such a way that they acquire reasoning and thinking skills. Wegerif and Dawes (2004) describe a programme of teaching children to talk profitably by practising these skills when working together in small groups at a computer. Such a programme would be equally relevant for any group or paired work. They suggest that children not only need to be taught listening skills but also how they might consider other people's suggestions, listening carefully and looking for positive ways of developing them, or perhaps suggesting ways of exploring someone else's ideas or questioning them further so that they develop their thinking. The idea is that the group tries to reach a consensus by exploring all aspects of the suggestions made and reasoning out why one suggestion is better than another. When a question is asked of the class, it helps to generate more thoughtful answers if children discuss it with a partner before answering. This is another way in which children can develop their thinking skills.

There is also a case for encouraging reflection on experience. A group, when they have arrived at a conclusion, can be asked to consider how effective they have been in working together. If you discuss with them before the discussion starts what they might look out for, they can refer back to this at the end of the discussion. They need to be concerned about whether people were encouraged to contribute, whether silent members were asked for their views, whether they tried to develop other people's ideas, whether they all contributed to a consensus.

There is also a case, with groups of older children, for appointing or getting them to appoint a leader and to consider his or her role. There should be discussion about the skills of discussion leadership before the groups go into action, so that everyone knows what the leader is supposed to do. A good discussion leader encourages members of the group to contribute, notes those who are not contributing and brings them into the discussion by asking them for a view. S/he tries to build on individual contributions by commenting positively on what each person has said and trying to build further on it, summing up at intervals and at the end of the discussion and trying to move the discussion on. The group might then spend time at the end discussing how they did and where the leader did particularly well.

Citizenship

Citizenship is a recent addition to the curriculum and is not compulsory at the primary stage although there are many aspects that may be introduced.

It can very often be useful to use occasions when there are particular events taking place, such as elections, that can be discussed. In one school where the school hall was being used as a polling station the teacher of Year 6 took the opportunity to arrange for them to be shown the arrangements for the election at a time when not many people started coming in to vote. The children watched a few people voting. They enjoyed this experience and learnt a good deal from it. They went on to talk about the purposes for which people were elected – for members of parliament or for local councils. This led to more discussion of the organisation of parliament, the political parties, the roles of the

Prime Minister and other ministers and the opposition parties. They then went on to look at local government and the roles involved.

Children can also learn something about democracy from having a school council to which children are elected to represent different age groups.

Atmosphere, attitudes and values

The ethos of the school has an effect on all its members. An effective school has an atmosphere of encouragement and a 'you can do it' outlook that requires both children and teachers to aim high and work to achieve demanding goals. Hard work is valued and it leads to good results. Each child is cared for as an important individual who has something to contribute. Good relationships are valued and much is done to teach children how to get on well with other people. Good behaviour is rewarded with attention and praise.

Dealing with bullying

Bertha was the class teacher of Year 4, and she was a bit disturbed when a child, Jessie, came to her and said she was being bullied by a group of girls in the class. Apparently they waited for her at playtime and after school and called her names and pushed her into puddles and threw her belongings into the gutter. She did not want to say who they were for fear of reprisals, but she said that there were four of them and that she often went home crying. Her mother was worried about her and told her to tell her teacher.

Bertha thought about the best way of dealing with this and concluded that she would deal with it in circle time and see if she could prevent it by talking with the children about how bullying made them feel. She started by asking whether anybody had been bullied and was a bit surprised to find that two girls and two boys put up their hands. She asked each of them to say how being bullied made them feel. They said it made them feel unhappy and two said it made them cry. They felt hurt that other people should dislike them so much that they attacked them. They said they thought about it in bed at night and imagined how they could do something unpleasant to the children concerned.

Bertha asked the others whether they were happy that some people were being made miserable by others and asked what they thought should be done about it. To start off with, various unpleasant consequences for the bullies were suggested, but Bertha said that this might simply make them more careful not to be found out, which might mean that they would torment bullied children even more to force them to say that they would not tell. It would not change them so that they stopped being unkind to others.

Bertha talked a bit about the need to be kind to others and help them if they were in trouble. She suggested that they should choose some children – both girls and boys – who would make themselves responsible for looking after children who were being bullied and would do all they could to prevent bullying happening, reporting it to the teacher if they saw someone having a bad time.

She asked who would be willing to do this and a number of children put up their hands. She put their names on the board and asked the class to vote for two girls and two boys from this list. She arranged to meet them in the lunch hour and talked to them about how to do this job. She gave them special badges to wear and told the class that anyone who was being bullied should go to one of the children wearing a badge and ask for help. This might be a matter of reporting it to the teacher on duty or to the class teacher.

This seemed to work quite well. Later in the term she asked whether anyone was being bullied and no one put up a hand.

Feelings are important. Do we do enough to help children with feelings of inferiority? Do we encourage and enable children to talk about their feelings and what causes unhappy or uncomfortable feelings? Do we do enough to make children aware of the feelings they can cause in others, both children and adults?

At all stages teachers are concerned to teach children the skills of thinking and learning, always aiming for independent learning. By Year 6 most children should be able to choose a topic or to work at one chosen for them, plan the work, research it using books and the internet, decide which are the most relevant pieces of information for the task in hand and compile and present the work effectively in writing or as an illustrated computer presentation, a verbal presentation or any other form of presentation that the child thinks suitable. They can also do this in pairs or groups.

The personal, social and health education programme

This subject has been singled out from the curriculum in this chapter because it is has a part to play in all the life and work of the school. The development of good personal relationships is an essential life skill and is important also for the development of a positive self-image. Relationships affect all aspects of schooling and determine the quality of education each child receives. The programme followed must be defined and given proper attention rather than being regarded as something that is done incidentally as the need arises – although this should also happen.

Questions to think about

1 Have we a defined programme with time set aside for PSHE?
2 Do we evaluate its effectiveness as often as we do the mathematics or English programmes? What criteria do we use?
3 How effective are our children as communicators? In speech? In writing or other forms of presentation?
4 Do we choose to teach sex education in our school? If so, what do we actually teach? Does it pose any problems?
5 Do we help children both to manage their own feelings and to be concerned about the feelings of others?
6 How successful are we at helping our children to become independent learners?
7 Are we developing in children the ability to work collaboratively in pairs or small groups?
8 What are we doing about citizenship education? What is it appropriate to teach at each stage?
9 How successful are we at helping children to form good relationships with others?
10 Do we demonstrate high expectations for all our children and help them to aim high?

Chapter 11

Working with support staff and volunteers

Benefits of working with support staff

Most teachers nowadays have the help of support staff who contribute to the work of schools in a variety of ways. All schools now have help with various administrative tasks, help with children with special needs and help in the classroom. Some schools may also have some volunteer help from parents and others. This help makes it much more possible to personalise learning for children and provide for the needs of individuals. It makes it possible to delegate routine tasks such as mounting work for display, preparing materials and resources and ensuring that they are kept in good condition and order ready for use. It increases the adult/child contact and makes it possible to provide more individual attention, support and encouragement to those who need it and cuts down queuing for your attention. It makes it possible to observe and record children's progress more fully. Having more adults available enhances and helps to provide a more interesting curriculum because more ideas are available.

The school may also have LSAs who will work with the school SENCO to provide support for children with special educational needs. They will give help to individual children in your class and bring ideas and suggestions for ways in which such children can be helped.

Appointing an assistant

You may be in a position to help in appointing an assistant, and this means starting by thinking out how you want to work and the skills and abilities you will be looking for in making an appointment. The first task will be that of drawing up a job description. If your school already has a number of assistants of various kinds there will probably be a standard job description, but you may be able to add to it to include tasks that are particularly relevant to your class.

An important element in making such an appointment will be the opportunity to meet the applicants informally to see whether they are people with whom you think you could work well. You want someone who is really interested in children and preferably has some experience with them, perhaps as a parent or as a volunteer. Look for a person who has ideas about helping children to learn, perhaps with experience of helping his or her own children with their school work. You want someone who is patient and calm with a slow learner or a child who is being difficult. Find out all you can about previous employment or experience. Someone who has clerical experience may be able to help by typing or assisting children using a computer. A person with organising experience may be useful at organising aspects of classroom life. All sorts of skills are useful in the classroom, and discussion of how these might be used will provide a good starting point for an assistant.

If you are a SENCO looking for LSAs you will be looking for someone with much the same sorts of skills and experience as well as a particular interest in children who have learning difficulties. In both situations a person who is interesting to adults may be equally interesting to children.

You may be able to find out this kind of information during a relaxed discussion before an interview or you may be looking for it while taking part in an interview. Work out before the interview the questions you want to ask. If you have had discussion with the candidate prior to the interview, you may want to ask questions that draw out the things that interested you in that discussion in order to make them clear to your fellow interviewers.

Team work

Much depends on how well you are able to work with your supporters and your relationship with them. You need to work as a team. This means that you, as the teacher and the leader of the team, need to have a clear idea of what each person has to offer and plan so that the contributions fit together. You will also need to train your supporters so that they can play a helpful part in the work of the class and so that as a team you can achieve more than you could alone. If you are a SENCO, you will need to make similar plans, although in this case, LSAs will have to work with class teachers as well as with you.

At an early stage you need to agree clearly exactly what your assistants may do without reference to you and the areas in which they should always refer to you. They will want to know how far you want to vet their plans in advance. You will probably want to do this in some detail until you know one another well. You will need to make clear exactly what the assistant is responsible for. Is s/he responsible for preparing resources and what does this involve? What should s/he do if a child misbehaves? What should s/he do if a child asks to go to the toilet? Provide plenty of opportunities for the assistant to ask questions and to make suggestions about ways of doing things. Try to provide a certain amount of freedom in ways of setting about things within an agreed framework.

One area in which an assistant should be clear about what to do is in relation to parents. Make it clear that the picture a parent gets of what goes on in school should be agreed and that the assistant needs to be careful about confidentiality. While it is important that the school gives parents an honest and full account of their children's progress, it should be a considered account with some emphasis on what the school is doing to support the child and what the parent can do to help. Teaching assistants usually live locally and will have friends among the parents. It is all too easy for bits of information to be dropped casually and give a biased picture of what is happening in school. This should be discussed with teaching assistants at an early stage.

Both teaching assistants and LSAs have to learn how to work with children. They will learn from watching teachers at work and you can help by discussing what you are doing when you work with the class and how you deal with misbehaviour. An assistant will learn if you suggest things to observe and discuss them afterwards. This can often be useful to you too. For example, you might ask an assistant to note how you explained something to a child or children, the sorts of comments you make on their work when you move round the class looking at what individuals are doing. Talk over ways in which the assistant might work with a group and at a later stage discuss the assistant's ideas about this when s/he tries to put it into practice. Talk over ways in which the assistant might work with a group, and at a later stage discuss what happened. Find occasions to discuss the assistant's ideas about approaching a particular piece of work and review what happened afterwards.

Record keeping

Teaching assistants can contribute to records of the children's work and progress. This will be helpful to the assistants as well as to you. It will help them to become skilled in noting relevant development, which will help to add to their knowledge of the children

Supporting an assistant

Monica was the class teacher of Year 3 and had as an assistant Hannah Jones, a young and enthusiastic girl who had been very helpful in organising resources and putting up displays. Monica got on well with her and they worked well together. A problem that came to light gradually as Hannah worked with more children was that she appeared to have some difficulty in managing them. Her groups tended to be noisy, and she frequently referred children to Monica because they would not do what she wanted. Monica tried her best to support her but the situation did not seem to improve.

The matter came to a head in Monica's mind when a small boy, Robin, who was something of a slow learner, came to her and said, 'Need I be in Miss Jones's group any more? I don't think I'm getting on very well.' Monica talked this over with Hannah and asked how she felt about it. It became clear that Hannah was getting really depressed about her inability to manage children. Monica decided that she must do some close observation of what was happening. She appreciated that if she simply sat and watched a group, her presence would affect how the children behaved, and she thought the best way to help would be to record on tape what happened when Hannah was working with a group, so that she could look out for anything that led to problems. They could listen to the tape together afterwards and see if Monica could pin down any reasons for the problems.

The tape was very revealing. Hannah started by talking for quite a long time before she involved the children. She had prepared well, but the children were not responding to her. They were reluctant to answer questions and when Monica listened to Hannah's responses to such replies as were offered, she began to see the extent of the problem. Hannah never appeared to praise and frequently found fault with what the children said. She never built on their replies or encouraged them to develop ideas further. She was never encouraging and was frequently dismissive of what the children volunteered. The outcome of this approach was that the children were bored and restless and unready to contribute, and they turned their attention to disruptive ploys.

Monica felt she had offered Hannah a good deal of praise and encouragement herself and had never directly criticised, preferring to offer suggestions about a different way of doing things. She asked Hannah how she would feel if the situation were reversed, and she was never offered praise and encouragement, only criticism. Hannah said she had not thought of the problem in this light. She said she was following the example set by some of the teachers she had experienced at her own school and agreed that such an approach was not very encouraging. They talked over the material on the tape and tried to think of different ways in which Hannah might have dealt with the children's responses. Monica also suggested that Hannah talked for too long before giving the children something to do. She needed to bring in something practical at an earlier stage and fit in some of what she wanted to say at a later stage and keep each contribution short. Hannah found this really helpful and started to put it into practice. Things did not change overnight, but she gradually persuaded the children that they would not be criticised unhelpfully for the answers they volunteered and the situation became much easier. She also varied the pattern of the work so that children were active more quickly.

and see more clearly what to do next with them. You will need to agree the records you would like kept. If you are working with a young class you will want records of each child's reading progress to be added to each occasion your assistants hear a child read. Assistants will need to look out for things such as the child's ability to self-correct, to work out new words from their phonic components, the child's understanding of the text being read and ability to read with expression. With slightly older children assistants might look for the ability to make inferences from the text and predict what might be coming next. In mathematics you might ask for knowledge of tables to be recorded or a child's facility or difficulty with certain types of sums. You might also want a record of how well a child has understood work done with the class. You could agree that your assistants have a file with a page for each child on which they enter anything that seems relevant about the child's progress or difficulties. The pages could eventually become part of the class record along with your own records.

Professional development

Assistants, like teachers, should be continually developing their work, and you will be important in helping this development. The tasks you give them and the discussions you have about children's progress and how to ensure it, will develop your assistants' skills and increase the contribution they can make to the work in hand.

There are now opportunities for assistants to gain qualifications in their work. There are National Vocational Qualifications (NVQs) that can be gained with courses leading to these offered by further education colleges, and teaching assistants should be encouraged to study for them. Assessment will be partly based on assessment of the work the assistant is doing in the classroom. More advanced NVQ qualifications can lead to higher level assistants' posts.

Part of the assistants' development will come through the school's performance management system where teaching assistants as well as teachers have their work observed and assessed regularly. This is followed by a discussion about the observation and the making of plans for future development, perhaps setting targets to be achieved in a given period. This is also an opportunity to air any concerns assistants may have about their work and the professional development opportunities they would like.

Volunteers

In addition to teaching assistants, you may also have some help from volunteers, usually parents, who are willing to help. Your teaching assistants are paid for their work and the volunteers work for free, so it will be important to make a clear distinction between the tasks you ask volunteers to undertake and those undertaken by teaching assistants. The volunteer may have less to do with children's learning than a teaching assistant. An exception to this might be hearing children read and perhaps reading to a small group. Volunteers may also be helpful in such tasks as getting children changed for physical education. They may be helpful in preparing resources and tidying up. Volunteers may also do a useful job in the school library, seeing that books are returned to the right place, perhaps helping with cataloguing or displaying books.

However, many of the things that apply when working with teaching assistants also apply when working with volunteers. You need to be very clear about the boundaries of the job and the support the volunteer can expect from you.

Questions to think about

1   What qualities should I look for when appointing an assistant?
2   Has the person being considered any particular skills or experiences that would be useful? Can s/he type? Is s/he good at organising? Has s/he artistic or musical ability or skill in sports?

continued

3   What tasks do I want to delegate to my assistant? What will be involved in this delegation? How can we work together most profitably?

4   How can I best train my assistant so that s/he works effectively?

5   Have I made it clear what my assistant can do independently and what s/he needs to refer to me? What support can s/he expect from me?

6   Is my assistants clear about what his or her relationship with parents should be? Does s/he understand the confidentiality that is necessary?

7   What records do I want him or her to keep?

8   Am I encouraging my assistant to look at the possibility of further training?

9   If I have help from volunteers as well as teaching assistants, am I clear about the differences between their roles?

Chapter 12

Working with parents

Parents have an important part to play in the education of their children. They have been responsible for much of the child's early learning and need to be encouraged to support their children through the foundation and later stages of education. Partnership is the relationship to aim for, with a two-way discussion over many aspects of the child's development. Parents have a more intimate knowledge of their children than teachers and can do much to support the work of the school if they are sufficiently involved. At the foundation stage parents are usually in daily contact with their child's teachers, meeting them as they bring their children to school and collect them in the afternoon.

Teachers have much to learn from parents at all stages. In particular teachers can get a view of the child at home and his or her interests and developing skills, which can inform their teaching and help them to match work appropriately to individuals. In some areas there will be a problem for teachers wanting to learn from parents. Teachers may not speak the language of the parents, and parents may not speak English. If there are EMAG teachers or other interpreters, teachers should take advantage of this facility whenever they can. They also need to use such opportunities to seek to understand the family culture.

Communication

Another barrier may be a lack of confidence on the part of parents, who may perhaps lack education themselves and have a view of teachers as people who know everything. This may make them hesitate to talk freely to teachers. Some teachers, for their part, may underestimate such parents and feel there is little purpose in talking with them. Both parents and teachers should seek to overcome these barriers, but the onus is on the teacher to make and use opportunities to explain things to the parents and draw them out about their views.

Good communication between teachers and parents is very important. Parents have a contribution to make to the education of their children, and there is a real need for teachers and parents to share information so that the child gets the best possible chance of success. Teachers need to listen to parents both individually and in meetings, and there should be plenty of opportunities for discussion throughout the primary years. Parents can be encouraged to come into the school, perhaps to observe what goes on, to meet and talk with their child's teacher and to help in some way. Open days are useful, although provision must be made for parents who are in full-time employment and are therefore unable to come into the school when it is in session. Most schools try to arrange for parents to come to an evening meeting when there is a chance to talk over their child's work and behaviour with his or her teacher. Teachers should try to make this a two-way discussion and use the opportunity to learn as much as possible from the parents about the child at home. The parents too need the opportunity to learn from the teachers about the child at school. Feedback on the child's work should be as positive as possible, identifying areas where the parents could help the child to make progress. Targets agreed with children should be shared with the parents and suggestions made as to how they could help at home.

Developing work with parents

Richard had just been appointed as head of a two-form-entry primary school. At his interview he was asked a lot of questions about relationships with parents, and he guessed that his predecessor had rather neglected this area of work. This was confirmed when he took up the post and various parents came to see him, asking him to make the school more parent-friendly. Staff confirmed that parents were kept at arm's length by the previous head and he decided to make parent relationships a major project for his first year in post.

He started by inviting parents to a meeting to talk about what he was planning. He said that he wanted much more parent involvement than had been the case in the past and he asked the parents who came to the meeting what they would welcome by way of involvement. He found them very receptive. They would like to know much more about their children's progress and about the programme the school was following. They wanted to know how they could help their children and if there were ways in which they could do more to help the school. They would like more opportunities to talk with their child's teacher and to hear about the work that was being planned and in progress.

It became very clear to Richard that there was a good deal to be done and he discussed this with the staff. Some of the older members, who had worked for a long time with the previous head teacher, were not keen to change the situation too drastically, but were willing to discuss possibilities. Some of the younger teachers were enthusiastic about such changes, especially those who had their own children in the school.

They talked about what they could do. Richard suggested that they should revive the parent/teacher association (PTA) so that they could discuss with parents what they would like to happen. It had fallen into abeyance over the years and they agreed that they needed a group with whom they could discuss developments. They also suggested a parents' newsletter to go out each half-term, giving information about what was happening. They could have a parents' notice board on which both staff and parents could post notices. The deputy head suggested that they could make a parents' room out of a partially disused storeroom. This would give a base for the PTA committee to meet, and parents could be involved with helping the staff with tasks such as cutting up paper and repairing books and equipment.

These suggestions were all met with enthusiasm on the part of parents and with general acceptance by the staff. A number of parents expressed themselves willing to help in any way they could, and this offer was taken up enthusiastically by the school. By the end of Richard's first year in headship the PTA was flourishing and there were numbers of parents volunteering to help with different things. The staff gradually came to value their help and recognised how much they could learn about the children from discussions with parents.

Good communication with parents starts when the child is admitted to the school. There may have been opportunities for parents and child to visit before entry and it will be very important for parents and child to be made welcome and be reassured about what will happen at school. Meeting the child's teacher will be the start of a relationship for both parents and child and it is an opportunity for the parents to tell the teacher about their child. What are his or her likes and dislikes? What is s/he interested in? What does s/he do at home or what has s/he done in pre-school? What does s/he know? What does s/he enjoy? Can s/he count? Does s/he recognise numbers and letters? Is s/he interested in books?

This is also an opportunity for the teacher to learn about the family. How many children are there and where does this particular child come? How old are the child's siblings? Is the child generally healthy? What illnesses has the child had? It is also an opportunity to assess the contribution the parents might be able to make. Do they read to the child regularly? What things do they do together? What have they tried to teach the child to do and with what success? What are their expectations of the school?

Parental contributions

All parents can make some contribution to their child's education. With younger children they can read to them, pointing out some of the common words and asking them to find another example. As children start to recognise more words they can be encouraged to follow a parent's reading of a text. It is a good idea to tell parents about the way they teach reading in the school so that the parent can contribute to the work of the teacher. Parents can next be encouraged to hear their children read regularly, perhaps using books lent by the school if there are not suitable books at home. It is a good idea to talk to parents about hearing reading, suggesting what to do if the child hesitates over a word and stressing the need to be encouraging and to offer praise whenever possible. Research suggests that this is a valuable contribution to the child's learning. It is particularly valuable if fathers will help their sons read. Boys need to see that men read as well as women and it is a good idea to try to involve fathers in their children's education.

Parents can also encourage children to count things and do practical sums such as 'How many spoons do we need to put on the table for lunch?', 'How many spoons would we need if Grandma and Grandpa came to lunch?' or 'There are twelve chocolates in a box and four children in the family. How many chocolates would each child get if the chocolates are shared out equally?'

The school needs to help parents to see ways in which they can help their children. Some of the differences in achievement between children from different social backgrounds come about because some parents are more concerned than others about their children's learning and do more to provide learning opportunities at home. The school needs to do all it can to encourage parents to help their children to learn, especially working-class parents who may lack confidence in their ability to help.

You will almost certainly have some children with special educational needs, and it will be important for parents to accept this and try to help such children at home. The school needs to identify ways in which parents can help and supply materials if necessary. It is equally important to identify ways in which parents can help very able children, talking with them about possible ideas that they can use.

As children grow older the school will encourage them to do homework, and it is important that parents support this practice. Parents may need some advice on this, especially where a very bright child comes from a working-class family. It is a good idea to send parents a statement about homework giving the purpose of it and suggesting ways in which parents can support the school in ensuring that homework gets done.

There may be parents who have particular skills that they would be happy to offer to the school. One parent may be keen on acting and would be prepared to help with a school production. Another may be a singer who would enjoy helping with a school choir. When the school makes the effort to get to know the parents as individuals, all sorts of opportunities may occur.

Reporting on children

Schools need to report to parents regularly on the progress of their children. These reports should be as positive as possible and be followed up by a meeting between the child's teacher and his or her parent(s) to discuss ways in which the child's work could be developed further, what the school will do to develop it and ways in which the parents could contribute. It is also an opportunity to discuss problems. Has the child special educational needs? Is the child very able? What is the school doing about it and what can the parents do? The meeting also gives an opportunity for parents and teachers to get to know each other better and, through such discussion, be better placed to help the child.

Questions to think about

1 Is our relationship with parents one of partnership?

2 Are we making opportunities to learn from parents about their children?

3 Have we a problem of parents who do not speak English? How can we communicate with these parents?

4 Do any of our parents lack confidence in speaking to teachers? What can we do to reassure them so that we can learn from each other?

5 How often do parents come into the school? Do they feel welcome? Do we listen to them sufficiently?

6 Do we provide opportunities for parents and children to visit the school before the children are admitted, so that they both can be reassured?

7 What contributions do parents make to the school? Are there ways in which they could contribute more? Have we parents who have skills that we could use?

8 Do we encourage parents to hear their children read regularly? Do we offer them any advice on doing this?

9 What information about the school do we offer parents? Do we send out newsletters?

10 Do we follow up school reports with a meeting to discuss the child's progress?

Chapter 13

Staff development

If a school is to make learning personalised it needs to ensure that staff – both teachers and teaching assistants – are involved in appropriate development programmes. This should be a continuing process, much of which can be part of the normal work of the school alongside a planned programme of training.

The professional development coordinator (PDC)

The first requirement is that the head teacher and the senior staff are committed to staff development for themselves and for others and continually seek ways of developing people. An important role in helping the school to become a professional learning community is that of the professional development coordinator (PDC). This person should be well informed about ways in which teachers and assistants can develop their work. S/he should be aware of the professional development needs of each member of staff – teaching assistants as well as teachers – and be in touch with professional development opportunities available locally. The head will, of course, want to be involved in all professional development plans, and the PDC will need to work closely with him or her, whether concerning a teacher's or an assistant's attendance at a course or planning for professional development meetings (PDMs) or in-service days. The PDC should be able recommend ideas for in-service days, perhaps suggesting speakers or particular activities that might be used.

The PDC may also link members of staff who share particular interests and suggest ways in which they might work together and share ideas. S/he may be able to recommend teachers who have ideas and practices that might be more widely shared. The Primary Strategy involves developing a 'raising attainment plan' (RAP) in literacy and numeracy for the whole school. All the staff, including teaching assistants, then have regular half-termly PDMs at which staff discuss plans for the coming half-term and agree targets for their work, chosen by individual teachers to fit in with the school's RAP targets for the half-term.

The PDC will have a key role in organising the RAP and may be able to make suggestions about the school's regular half-termly PDMs, if the school works in this way. S/he may act as scribe for such meetings, providing the agenda (in consultation with the head) and taking the minutes, recording the targets that each teacher decides to set and also some of the discussion. The overall programme should involve a large number of people learning from each other, by discussion and observation.

The professional development meetings

The meetings give the staff opportunities to share ideas about successful practice, and it is suggested that each teacher agrees not more than three targets in literacy and mathematics for his or her class, thinking particularly about children who are underperforming. There would also be a case for thinking about targets for the most able, although this is not part of the Primary Strategy. Teachers then discuss ways of teaching to achieve these targets, sometimes working in year group teams where the school is large enough to have more than one class in a year group.

The target-setting should involve stating what children should learn and what the outcomes should be, the whole forming an IDP for the teacher. In smaller schools the discussion may be more general with the head teacher asking teachers who have worked particularly successfully at some aspect to talk to the others about it. The discussion gives teachers the opportunity to think about different ways of planning and teaching and about how best to involve children in their learning. The literacy and numeracy coordinators may contribute to the discussion and plan a programme of support where teachers wish for, or appear to need this.

At a subsequent meeting to prepare for the next half-term, each teacher will report on what s/he has done, what seemed to be successful, what was less successful and any areas where s/he could do with support. Problems will be discussed and plans made for the next half-term.

The emphasis here will be on what can be learned from successes, and the difficulties and the problems people have encountered can be discussed, solutions suggested and help offered where it is needed.

Classroom practice

This programme requires teachers to share their objectives with the children at the beginning of a lesson. It is also a good idea to explain why they are learning about a particular topic and how it fits into a bigger picture. They need to be made aware of what they will be able to know, understand or do at the end of the lesson and what they will do during it. This helps them to make sense of their own learning.

The Primary Strategy suggests that individual work should support children in drawing out patterns or conclusions and justifying relationships and that there should be some social interaction as children learn so that they learn from discussing work with each other (see p. 78: Working together).

Other ideas for staff development

A useful activity that the PDC might arrange in preparation for professional development meetings is for members of staff to do some reading on a topic that everybody wants to know about and then report to a staff meeting on it, perhaps providing a short summary of important points. It is also useful for different teachers to visit other schools and report back. One school used an in-service day by getting every member of staff to visit another school to observe what they did about an agreed topic, which was something their school wanted to develop. They then reported back to a staff meeting. They all found their visits extremely helpful, giving them all lots of ideas for introducing the same thing in their school. This kind of activity is especially helpful when a school is planning to introduce something new that is part of the practice elsewhere.

The PDC may also need to organise opportunities for discussing teaching and learning issues that are concerning the staff at any given time. Sometimes it may be a good idea to give a teacher the opportunity to air a particular problem s/he is facing for discussion by others. Teachers can learn a great deal from each other and it is desirable to create a situation in which this is regarded as a good thing to do fairly frequently. Another way of doing this is to hold meetings in each classroom in turn, giving the teachers of each class a chance to talk about the work on display and the ways in which s/he organises his or her work.

Head teachers can also provide learning opportunities both by observing teaching and giving feedback themselves and by providing some opportunities for teachers to observe each other, having first decided on what the teacher being observed would like as feedback.

Working together

Melanie and Pat were two enthusiastic young teachers who taught parallel Year 4 classes in a junior school. They were great friends and worked together whenever they could. Their school had adopted the ideas of the Primary Strategy and held half-termly meetings to discuss the way ahead. One spring term, they decided that one of their literacy targets would be for children to recognise parts of speech and know how nouns, verbs, adjectives and adverbs could be recognised and their different functions in sentences. These parts of speech came in different forms and the children would learn to recognise these and know what they signified. They would each teach the lesson they had planned with their class and compare notes about it before going on to develop the theme further.

They agreed that they would start their lessons by telling children what they had planned and that by the end of their lessons on parts of speech they would be able to recognise nouns, verbs, adjectives and adverbs and probably other kinds of words as well. They would also try to involve an element of problem-solving in the lessons.

They first prepared a series of sentences that they could project onto the whiteboard. These sentences contained verbs in the present tense and these were underlined. The children were asked what the words underlined had in common. The children went down several blind alleys before concluding that all the words were about doing something. (Melanie and Pat had been careful not to include the verb 'to be' in the sentences). They asked the children for more examples and soon the class seemed to have a fairly clear idea about verbs. They then did a similar exercise in identifying nouns.

They next gave the children a set of sentences that included past, present and future verbs and asked the children to discuss with a partner how these verbs were different and what the difference was. This took a little time, but the children got there in the end. They then did a similar exercise with nouns, giving singular and plural forms and including different ways of signifying this. The children grasped this immediately.

When it came to the time for individual work they gave children a series of verbs (infinitives) and asked them write sentences with these first in the past tense and then in the future tense. This gave them a chance to discover how well the children had achieved the target for the lesson. Overall the children seemed to have absorbed the ideas, and they were able to go on and plan further work on parts of speech.

Discussion by pairs of teachers following observation of each other's work can be very enlightening. It is not altogether easy to provide such opportunities in a primary school, but if the head is not a class teacher and is willing to step in to take a class, or to provide for a supply teacher for a day, it is a possibility.

Another opportunity of this kind is team teaching. Two classes can work together on an agreed theme with both their teachers, perhaps in the school hall. This gives each teacher an opportunity to see the other teach, and they can share ideas and conclusions.

There are many informal ways of providing development opportunities, and if it can be agreed that people have a lot to learn from each other, they can very effective. In addition, there should be more formal opportunities, such as the PDMs. Teachers should be encouraged to go to courses on relevant subjects and to report on this experience to colleagues. In-service days should be orientated to provide opportunities to discuss issues arising from trying to personalise learning for all children, for bringing in outside speakers and for arranging for different members of staff to plan the programme so that it covers areas that teachers want to hear about and discuss in relation to their own particular class. All members of staff, including teaching assistants, whatever their experience, should be involved in staff development.

One primary school arranged for all teachers to change places with a colleague for a day once a term so that they learned about the work of a different age group. The class teacher in each case provided lesson notes in advance so that the incoming teacher could prepare, and they then arranged to have a discussion afterwards about what happened. This enlarged the perspective of all the staff and gave teachers an idea of what work came before or after the work of their own class.

Contributions by subject leaders and leaders for different areas

Subject leaders in primary schools have a responsibility to help and support their colleagues within a subject, perhaps working with them when an opportunity can be found. In addition to the RAP there should be a scheme of work that the staff are following, usually drawn up by the subject leader in consultation with colleagues. There should be opportunities provided for each subject leader to talk about his or her subject as well as providing the scheme of work and suggesting ideas. It is also useful for the SENCO to talk about ways of helping children with special needs as well as helping individual teachers with individual children. The leaders of different groups (such as boys and girls, very able children, children from different cultures and social backgrounds), the SENCO and the subject leaders will all have something to contribute to in-service training, both formally and informally.

Relationships with parents

An important area that needs to be considered as part of staff development is that of relationships with parents. The school needs to have a policy about this that sets out the sorts of relationships that are desirable. The staff need to decide what information should be made available to parents, how this should be done and who should do it. The aim should be a partnership with parents that involves parents in their children's education and enables them to help to the best of their ability.

Performance management

The school performance management system should apply to all staff, including teaching assistants, and should include discussion of each person's learning needs. All staff should be encouraged to think about their learning needs on a regular basis, with the PDC surveying these regularly, perhaps by giving all staff a questionnaire about the areas in which they feel they would like further training. This information should then feed into the school planning for in-service days and for planning who might be given opportunities to attend external courses.

Questions to think about

1   What are we gaining from our professional development meetings and in-service days? What effect is this having on children's learning?
2   How effective is our evaluation and record-keeping system? What have we done to evaluate different aspects of our work?
3   Are the records we keep effective? Do we use them to seek ways to raise attainment?

continued

4   Do we record the conclusions when we do experimental work stemming from our PDMs?

5   How can we ensure that we all – teachers and teaching assistants – are involved and succeeding in raising attainment?

6   What part should subject leaders and leaders of areas such as working with children from other cultures play in overall staff development?

7   Are we doing as much as we can to learn from each other?

Chapter 14

School self-evaluation

Planning evaluation

There is a great deal involved in personalising learning for children, and the head teacher and all the staff need to keep a critical eye on all that the school is doing. Planning for evaluation needs to be considered at the same time as you plan your programme as a staff and individually, for the term or the year. Evaluation is easier if you have set clear targets for your work, as suggested in the previous chapters, and considered how and when progress towards them should be evaluated. Try to identify the questions you will want your evaluation to answer, both for the individual class and for the school more generally. These should be discussed at a staff meeting and agreement reached about who should be responsible for looking into each question and the ways in which this evaluation might be carried out. The overall plan should be agreed by all staff including teaching assistants. Your need to agree what will be included, the criteria to be used in judging the outcomes, who will do each part of the process and what will be done with the conclusions. The individual teacher also needs to think about how he or she will evaluate his or her work on a regular basis.

Your record-keeping becomes clearer if you consider how what you are recording will contribute to your overall evaluation and the school's overall evaluation as well as helping you to decide what to do next. It should not be forgotten that as well as the intended findings unexpected things will probably result from evaluation and that these should be noted so that they can be taken into account in future planning. It is particularly important to take note of negative findings as well as positive ones. Which bits of planning for personalisation did not work? Why was this? How could you avoid such failures next time?

Methods of evaluation

You next need to consider what evidence will be needed to answer each question and how it can be gathered. The head teacher has an important leadership role here in seeing that all staff are concerned to check regularly how they are doing.

Data collection

This means ensuring that there is regular collection and recording of data that can be scrutinised to see which questions it helps to answer and what can be learned from it. This needs to be done at a school level and at the level of the individual class, the individual teacher and the teaching assistant.

The data collected should include the outcomes of the targets set as part of the RAP, the results of tests, including SATs, class teachers' and teaching assistants' records, records kept by older children of their targets and achievements and teachers' records of these for younger children and notes of reading ages. All teachers should do a self-evaluation as part of their performance management and the head teacher should maintain a record of targets agreed with each teacher. Class teachers will be responsible for evaluating the work of any teaching assistants and the SENCO for LSAs.

It was suggested in an earlier chapter that each teacher should keep a file with a page for each child on which his or her progress across the board is recorded and notes made of discussions with each child as an individual, together with the targets agreed with the child and notes of his or her progress towards those targets. When a page is filled the sheet can be transferred to a file that is kept for that child, thus making a more permanent record. The older children themselves might keep record books, as suggested in Chapter 4, recording their views of how they have done and their targets for the future. These also offer useful data.

Observation

Some information will be collected easily from teachers' records, but evaluation of teacher performance will be a question for the head teacher who, with help from the deputy, will observe each teacher regularly and provide a report on what is seen. Teachers can also be helped with self-evaluation by observing each other at work, if it can be arranged, and discussing their work together so that they can learn from each other.

Observation is more effective if those observing have a clear idea of what they want to see. It is useful for teacher and observer to consider together the information that would be useful to the teacher being observed. Tallying of particular teacher behaviour can be useful. How often does the teacher make positive comments to children and how often negative ones? How does s/he explain work to children? How are questioning sessions managed? What is the teacher's response to children's answers? How does s/he manage children's behaviour? Another idea is to look at the part children play in the lesson, perhaps mapping the classroom and noting which children are given the chance to answer questions, which children volunteer information, which children appear to be involved in what the class is doing and which children appear to be day-dreaming or otherwise occupied.

Questionnaires

Questionnaires are a useful method of gathering information at the individual or personal level and they can be used with teachers, teaching assistants or children. Questions need to be carefully designed so that the results are easy to assess and not too complex. It is useful to use some questions where people have to grade aspects of their work on a five-point scale. Some questions should be open, giving scope for personal opinions, and some closed with a yes or no answer. In designing a questionnaire it is important to bear in mind how it will be analysed. It can be easy to attract answers from which it is hard to extract and classify information.

Interviews and discussions

A good deal of information can be collected through talking to individuals and groups. The head teacher should have a regular interview with each member of staff as part of performance management and this will give him or her a lot of useful information. Group discussions can also be useful, allowing an evaluator to explore further ideas that have come up in questionnaires or teacher observation.

Teaching assistants

Teachers should have a procedure for evaluating their teaching assistants' work, and the SENCO should have a procedure for evaluating the work of LSAs. There should be a

Evaluation of the work of the head teacher

Martin was head teacher of a two-form-entry junior school. Managing an appraisal system for the staff made him aware of the need to set up some way of appraising his own work. He could, of course ask the local authority primary adviser for her opinion or ask the governors, but on reflection he felt that the really important evidence would come from the teachers if he had the courage to ask for it. He decided that one way of doing this would be to ask for the opinions of teachers on a number of specific questions, for example:

* How far do you feel supported in your work? Would you like more support? In what areas would this be helpful?
* Are you happy with the general organisation of the school? Are there any areas where you would like to see changes?
* Are you happy with the information you are given about the work of the school? Are there areas in which you would like to know more?
* Is the documentation (policies, schemes of work, etc.) satisfactory and sufficient guidance for your work? Is there too much or too little?
* Are you happy with the discipline in the school? Are the school rules adequate and effective?
* Are there any changes you would like to see?

He decided to give these questions to teachers as a questionnaire to be completed anonymously and then to discuss the results at a staff meeting. The staff were happy to do this and gave mostly very positive replies, but one or two people were fairly critical about the general organisation of the school and made some useful suggestions that Martin felt would be worth pursuing.

He then decided that he would pursue a slightly different set of questions with his governors. He felt that governors would have opinions about the effectiveness of the communication they received about the school and any areas where they would like to know more. They would probably be aware of what some parents think of the school and this too would be useful feedback both for him and for the staff.

regular meeting – perhaps termly when an assistant is new in post and yearly when s/he is more experienced – in which teacher or SENCO and assistant meet to go over the assistant's work and discuss possible areas for development. This is also an opportunity for the assistant to suggest ways in which the teacher or SENCO could help his or her development.

Experimental work

It is also important to record the progress of any experimental work, whether an experiment in working in a certain way or an attempt to overcome a particular problem. This could be an individual project or one involving a partner or a group. A school should collect such reports and keep them filed so that they can be used to help others who want to try things out. At the start of such work, it is wise to set some targets so that you can assess the work in the light of what you intended and at the same time consider how the project might be evaluated and when. In assessing the outcome it may be a good idea to enlist the help of a colleague who has not been involved in the planning.

Other areas

A school also needs to assess its progress in a wider way. How good is the school's relationship with parents? What do parents think of the relationship? How effective are the school rules? Do any need to be modified or any added? How good is children's behaviour? Have we effective ways of dealing with children who pose problems because of their behaviour?

Timing evaluation

Evaluation needs to be both on-going and a process that takes place at regular intervals. On-going evaluation involves reflection on what is happening as it takes place. In any given lesson you will note as you go along elements of progress by individual children or by the class as a whole. Some children will show that they have grasped an idea or that they are thinking ahead and making progress at a personal level. It is not always possible to record such progress but on reflecting on the lesson, you may be able to remember and record the outstanding points for future reference, which will guide you in future planning. Your records will eventually contribute to more general evaluation at school level, and this needs to be borne in mind when making them. There should be some agreement at school level about what should be recorded by everyone. This kind of on-going reflection is an important aspect of your overall evaluation of your work and that of the children and contributes in due course to whole school evaluation.

Planning the evaluation

Whole-school evaluation needs to take place at agreed intervals, possibly once a year, with smaller evaluations in between. It should be agreed what the evaluation should involve, what the outcomes should be and the time that it will require for all concerned. It might involve evaluating a process, such as the RAP professional development programme, or an outcome, such as the effect of the appraisal system on the work of the staff. In each case it will be necessary to decide on the questions to be asked and the evidence needed. These should be discussed at a staff meeting so that everyone is clear what is involved, what his or her contribution will be and the date by which it will be required. There must also be agreement about who will put the final report together and to whom it will be given. The head or deputy might want to compile the final report, but there is something to be said for giving this task to different members of staff in turn, since there is much to be learned from doing it.

The last stage of evaluation is to consider what should be done about the findings. This, in many ways, is the most important element, since it gives purpose to the whole enterprise. The outcome maybe a staff development programme, perhaps planning further investigation or different forms of recording to make evaluation easier in future, a change in ways of doing things, experimental work in following up the findings and many other ideas, suggestions for which might be part of the final report.

The final report should go to all members of staff, including teaching assistants, and to the governors. It may be wise to set interim dates for each part of the report so that no one feels rushed at the last minute.

Questions to think about

1   What can we do to plan for evaluation?
2   What records do we keep that will be useful for evaluation? Can we do anything to make evaluation information easier to access?

continued

3   How often should we evaluate as a whole school?

4   How should we decide what questions we need to ask?

5   How do we involve all staff in the evaluation process? How do we divide up the work of evaluation so that no one is overloaded?

6   What should we do as a result of evaluation?

Chapter 15

Conclusion

Personalising learning is not an easy option for a teacher, but it is very worthwhile for the children. Each class in a primary school contains a very wide range of children, all of whom have individual interests, characteristics and learning styles, and a variety of previous experience and learning skills. It is nevertheless possible to personalise learning, given the support of colleagues and teaching assistants. It involves knowing the children in your class very well – their particular interests and abilities. It also involves very good planning, with clear aims for each lesson for the whole class and subsidiary aims for a number of individuals – perhaps for boys and girls, children with special needs, children from ethnic minorities, particularly those whose English is limited, and children from different social backgrounds. Sometimes you will need to aim to provide for a particular group while dealing with the others in more general terms and sometimes you may be able to provide for several groups, using a teaching assistant to work with one or two of them. There may also be help from an LSA who will be able to work with children with special educational needs.

A particular problem of personalised learning is how you keep track of the progress different children are making. You will need to encourage teaching assistants and LSAs to help with record-keeping for the children with whom they work, discussing with them what you want to know and what you want to record. With older children you will have written work to help you to assess how individuals are doing, but with the younger ones you will be depending mainly on reports from assistants and your own observations. The record books suggested in Chapter 4 are useful with the older ones. Your own observations and discussions with children, either individually or as a group, will give you a good deal of information.

The intensifying support programme of the Primary Strategy places considerable stress on developing the school as a professional learning community. This is a very important aspect of personalising learning. Teachers attempting to match learning to the very different needs of a wide range of children need to take every opportunity to share ideas with colleagues and to learn from each other. If the school has teachers in leadership roles for gender, special educational needs, very able children, children from ethnic minorities and children learning English as a second language as well as leaders for different aspects of curriculum, teachers should have a helpful source of information for the teaching of children with varying needs. The professional development meetings described in Chapters 2 and 13 are worth pursuing, even if you are not, as a staff, working to a RAP. Regular meetings to discuss targets for the next half-term and report on success in achieving the last half-term's targets are a valuable discipline for planning and evaluating and for sharing ideas.

References

Berkshire Education Committee (1997) *Pathways to Life*, Reading: Berkshire County Council.

Connolly, P. (2004) *Boys and Schooling in the Early Years*, London: Routledge.

Department for Education and Skills (2000) *Curriculum Guidance for the Foundation Stage*, London: DfES.

Department for Education and Skills (2001) *Special Educational Needs Code of Practice*, London: DfES.

Department for Education and Skills (2004) *Excellence and Enjoyment: Learning and Teaching in the Primary Years: Learning to Learn: Progression in Key aspects of Learning*, London: DfES.

Department for Education and Skills (1995) *The National Curriculum*. London: DfES.

Donaldson, M. (1978) *Children's Minds*, London: Fontana.

Gardner, H. (1983) *Frames of Mind: The Theory of Multiple Intelligences*, New York: Basic Books.

Goleman, D. (1996) *Emotional Intelligence: Why It Can Matter More Than IQ*, London: Bloomsbury.

Gross, M. (2004) *Exceptionally Gifted Children*, London: Routledge.

Hay Mcber (2000) *Research into Teacher Effectiveness: A Model of Teacher Effectiveness*, London: DfES.

Lang, P. (1988) *Thinking About Personal and Social Education in the Primary School*, Oxford: Blackwell.

London Development Agency (2004) *The Educational Experiences of Black Boys in London Schools*, a report by the Education Commission, London.

McGarrigle, J. and Donaldson, M. (1974) 'Conservation Accidents', *Cognition*, 3: 341–50.

Ofsted (2004) *Setting Targets for Pupils with Special Educational Needs*, Ofsted, HMI 751.

Piaget, J. (1952) *The Origins of Intelligence in Children*, New York: International Universities Press.

Thomas, G., Walker, D. and Webb, J. (1998) *The Making of the Inclusive School*, London: Routledge.

Tilstone, C. and Layton, L. (2004) *Child Development and Teaching Pupils with Special Educational Needs*, London: Routledge.

Wallace, B. (1983) *Teaching the Very Able Child*, London: Ward Lock Educational.

Wegerif, R. and Dawes, L. (2004) *Thinking and Learning with ICT; Raising Achievement in Primary Classrooms*, Didcot: RoutledgeFalmer.

Vygotsky, L. S. (1978) *Mind in Society: The Development of Higher Psychological Processes*, Cambridge MA: Harvard University Press.

Index

ability: exceptional 45–51; grouping by 36, 50
able children 12; very able 45–51
achievement of different cultural groups 54
acquiring learning skills 2
advice to parents 55
appointing support staff 67–8
appraisal: of head teacher 83; system 84
assessment: and evaluation 18–19, 56; methods
    of 81–2; by peers 34; planning 81; questions
    81; of reading 34 64; school self- 81–5;
    timing of 84; of the work of the head
    teacher 83
assistants: learning support (LSAs) 35, 36, 38;
    teaching 3, 18, 19, 31, 67–71
asylum-seeker 54; children 55
atmosphere 65
attention, positive and negative 54–5
attitudes and values 64, 65

background, effects of social 58–61
behaviour: 27; of Afro-Caribbean children
    54–5; of children 82; effects of 32; gender
    29–30; non-verbal 57; teacher 31, 82
benefits of working with support staff 67
Berkshire LEA personal and social education
    paper 63–4
bilingual teachers 56, 57
black: African children 29; Afro-Caribbean
    children 29, 52, 53, 54–5
body language 23
boys: middle-class 30; and reading 4, 5;
    working-class 30
boys': development 12; performance 29
boys and girls: encouragement for 48; provision
    for 29–34; ways of helping to achieve more
    32–3
boys' and girls' attitudes: 29, 48; to reading 32;
    subject preferences 33
bullying 37–8, 65

catchment area 58–9
catering for all abilities 59–60
child development 14–16
children: Bangladeshi 29; black African 29;
    black Caribbean 29; with disabilities 29–44;

gifted 45–51; middle-class 30; Pakistani 29;
    quiet 48; with special educational needs 12,
    35–44; working-class 29
children's: backgrounds 1, 12, 58–61; career
    aspirations 59; play 14; records 13
choice, the place of 2
circle time 23, 65
citizenship 64–5
classroom: behaviour 27; culture and climate
    24; display 26; practice 77; rules 11, 27
class teacher 38
communication: with parents 72, 73; skills 62,
    64
computers 26, 50, 64
concept development 20
conclusion 86
confidentiality and support staff 68, 71
Connolly, P. 58
consulting children 9
contribution of parents 74
coordinator: of literacy 77; of numeracy 77; of
    professional development 76, 78
creativity 2, 45, 48, 50
culture and climate 7, 8

data collection 81–2
dealing: with children's mistakes 16; with
    incorrect answers 24, 31
decision-making by children 1
Department for Education and Skills 63
developing work with parents 73
development: child 63–4; emotional 6, 11, 16,
    63; girls' 12; girls' and boys' 29–34,
    individual plans for 9; personal and social
    47, 63; physical 15; planning 8, social 14,
    15, 16, 38
differentiating work 2, 3, 35–6
disabilities: children with 35, 36
discussion 22, 23, 24, 82; leadership 64
display 26
Donaldson, M. 15

EAL children 56–7; teachers 56
effects of social background 58–61
EMAG staff 55, 56, 57, 72

emotional: dealing with problems 17–18; development 6, 11, 16, 63; intelligence 17
encouragement and praise 54
English as an additional language (EAL) 54, 55, 56–7
environment: learning 26
Ethnic Minority Achievement Grant (EMAG) 55
ethnic minorities 59; customs of 56
ethnic minority teachers 55–6
ethos of classes and school 10, 65
evaluation 18–19, 64; methods of 81–2; outcomes 84; planning 81, 84; school self- 81–5; timing of 84; of the work of the head teacher 83
exceptionally able children 45–51; accelerated promotion for 49; teachers' attitudes towards 48
expectations: effect of 18, 30; teacher 54
experience and learning 20; reflection on 64
experimental work: recording progress 83
exploration of ideas 64

feelings: dealing with 63, 66
finding out about children 13
fostering relationships between children with special needs and others 35, 36

Gardner, H. 17
gender: behaviour 29; gap 29–33
gifted children 45–51; who are difficult 48
girls': development 12; social pressure on 48
girls and boys 29–34
goal setting: by children 25
Goleman, D. 17
Gross, M. 49
group: formation 32; leadership 23, 47; work 22–3, 64
grouping: by ability 36, 50; advantages of ability grouping 37; disadvantages 37; mixed ability grouping 36

Hay McBer 24
head teacher 77, 81, 82, 83
hearing children read 33
hidden curriculum 8

ICT 3, 26, 50
inclusion: 7, 56; and integration 35–36
independence in learning 2, 21
Individual Development Plan (IDP) 9, 77
in-service days 78
integrating children with disabilities 36
interviews 82
investigation 21

knowledge of other cultures 52; other customs 52

Lang, P. 62
language: boys' and girls' use of 33; development 14, 15, 16
leadership 64; roles 86
learning: attitudes to 30–1; through discussion 22, 23; from each other 78; environment 26; and experience 20; motivation for 26; tables 37; through play 22; preferences 30–1; process 20; through reading 22; skills 21; styles 5, 15, 20, 30–1; and teaching 20–28
learning and teaching assistants 20–28
learning support assistants (LSAs) 38
listening 22, 23
Local Education Authority (LEA) 55
London Development Agency 54

McGarrigle, J. and Donaldson, M. 15
masculinity 30, 33, 59
middle-class: children 30, 58; parents 59
mindmaps 22
monitoring performance: of boys and girls 29
motivation for learning 26
multicultural: education 52; resources 53

National Curriculum 34, 38, 62
National Vocational Qualifications (NVQs) 70

objectives, sharing with children 77
observation: of able children 45; of teacher performance 82
observing: children 14, 15; other teachers 78
other cultures, children from 52–7

paired work 24
Pakistani children 53
parental: attitudes 36–7, 45; contributions to their child's education 74; support 74
parents: communication with 72, 73, 79; contribution of 72, 74; partnership with 72; relationship with 79; and support staff 68; working with 72–5
parent/teacher association (PTA) 73
peer assessment 34
performance management: of all staff 79, 82; of support staff 70
personalising learning 86
personal relationships 66
personal and social development 4
personal, social and health education (PSHE) 62–6
physical: abilities 46; development 15; disabilities 35, 36
Piaget, J. 15

planning: for individual children 25; for school
  improvement 8; work 21
positive: and negative comments 10, 19;
  teacher behaviour 24; teaching 26
praise and encouragement 26, 41, 63, 69, 74
preferences: of boys 30–1; of girls 30–1;
  learning 30–1
Primary Strategy 9, 24, 76, 77, 78, 86
professional development 76–80; for assistants
  70; meetings (PDMs) 9, 76–7
provision: for boys and girls 29–34; for
  children of exceptional ability 47;
  for children from other cultures 52–7;
  for children with SEN 35–44

Qualified Teacher Status for ethnic minority
  teachers 55
questioning 24, 26
questionnaires 82
quiet children 48

racial prejudice 52
racism 52, 55
raising attainment: of black children 55; plan
  (RAP) 76, 81
reading: assessment of 34; development 4, 5;
  learning through 22; records 33
record keeping 14, 56, 68, 69–70
reflection on experience 64
relationships with parents 79
reporting on children 74–5
resolving conflict 23
rewards: extrinsic and intrinsic 27
risk-taking 26–7, 30
role-models 36

scaffolding learning 27
school: and classroom rules 11, 27; self-
  evaluation 81–5
seating 24
self-assessment by children 50
self-esteem 1, 26–7, 35–7, 63; and motivation
  37
self-evaluation: of school 81–5; by teachers and
  other staff 37
self-image 17, 36–7, 63
setting 35–6
skills: of communication 62, 64; development
  4; of investigation 21–2; of learning 21; of

listening 64; of problem-solving 21–2; social
  5, 6, 16. 22–3; of thinking 21;
social: background 58–61; development
  14, 15, 16, 38; skills 5, 6, 16, 22–3
space, use of 5
special educational needs 35–44
special educational needs coordinator (SENCO)
  36, 38, 67, 68. 79, 82–3
staff development 9, 76–80
stages of development 12, 13, 14, 15
Standard Assessment Tasks (SATs)
stereotyping 53
structuring learning 20
subject leaders 79
support staff 67–71; and parents 68; working
  with children 68
supporting an assistant 69

tables, learning 37
target-setting 3, 4, 18–19, 37, 76–7, 81
teacher: attention 32; attitudes 24; behaviour
  31; effects 32; expectations 18, 30, 32;
  responses 31
teachers: black 54–5; bilingual 56, 57;
  cooperating 9; EAL 56
teaching: assistants 3, 18, 19, 31, 82–3;
  interactive 26; positive 26, 67–71
team teaching 78
team work 68
testosterone 30
thinking skills development 15, 21
Thomas, G., Walker, D. and Webb, J. 35

underachievement 49, 51

values 7
vision 7
visiting other schools 77
volunteers 67–71; tasks for 70
Vygotsky, L.S. 27

Wallace, B. 47, 48
Wegerif, R. and Dawes, L. 3, 64
whole-school approach 7–1
working-class: children 29, 58; parents 59;
  speech 60
working with parents 72–5
working with support staff and volunteers
  67–71